NOSTALGIA SPOTLIGHT ON THE TWENTIES

61e Année. No 20 .   Le Numéro : 1. fr. 50   Samedi 19 Mai 1923

LA VIE PARISIENNE

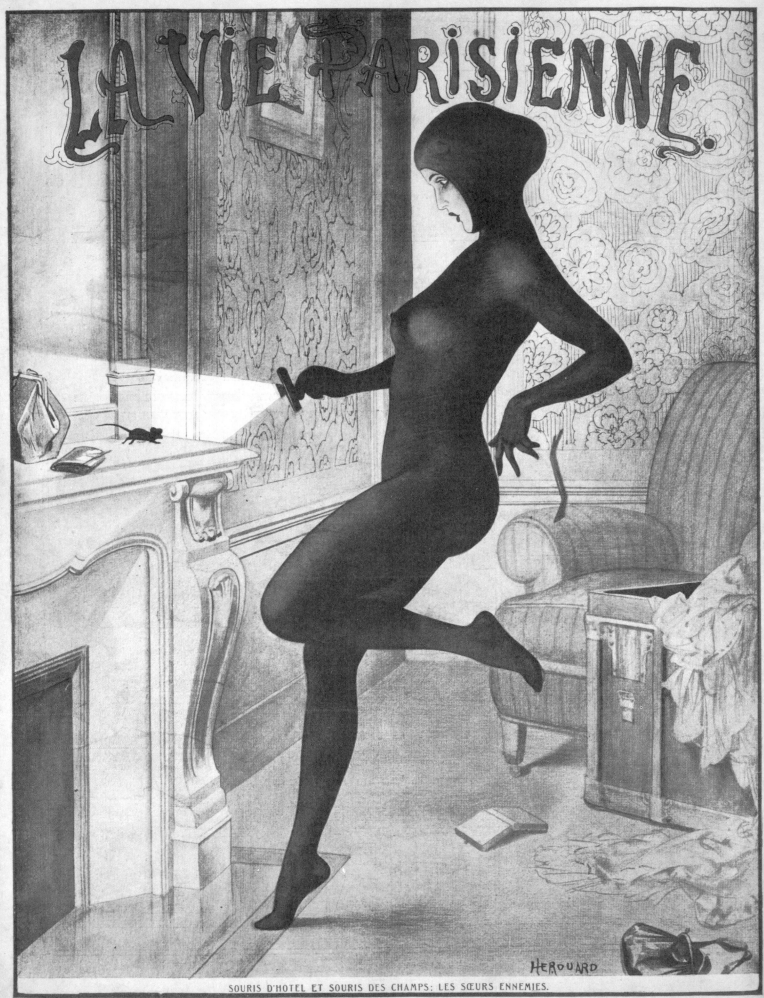

SOURIS D'HOTEL ET SOURIS DES CHAMPS: LES SŒURS ENNEMIES.

Rédaction, Administration et Publicité : 29, rue Tronchet, Paris.

NOSTALGIA SPOTLIGHT ON THE TWENTIES

Michael Anglo

First published in 1976 by
JUPITER BOOKS(LONDON) LIMITED
167 Hermitage Road, London N4 1LZ.

Copyright © Jupiter Books(London) Limited 1976

SBN 904041 47 6

This edition produced in 1985 by
Universal Books Ltd.,
The Grange,
Grange Yard,
London SE1 3AG

Composed on the Monotype
in 12/14pt Baskerville 169 by
HBM Typesetting Limited, Chorley, Lancashire.
Printed and bound by R. J. Acford
Chichester, Sussex.

41449

Contents

Blackbirds

I WAS JUST A KID WHEN I MET FLORENCE MILLS. IT WAS BACKSTAGE AT the London Hippodrome. *Blackbirds*, Lew Leslie's all-Negro review in which she starred, had hit London like a bomb, and my father was kept busy outfitting members of the cast. My father had been introduced to them by old friends, Scott and Whaley, the famous coloured British variety act. It was a good time for my family. For once we were in the chips.

My father became very friendly with many of the acts. For a number of years he continued to work for them and other acts, as well as bands who subsequently came to tour this country and to whom he had been recommended by members of the original *Blackbirds* cast. My mother did not like it too much when sometimes my father would go on tour with his friends while she stayed at home with her sons, especially as she did not approve of my father having taken to shooting craps with some of his cronies.

I met many showbiz people at the time, backstage at their hotels and at home when my parents entertained them. The names that stick in my mind are Cab Calloway, Noble Sissle, Louis Armstrong and the immaculate Pegleg Bates, the one-legged dancer who appeared in *Porgy and Bess*. There was the comedian, Johnny Hudgins, quiet and friendly, who bought me a book for a present, Lamb's *Tales from Shakespeare*. He told me to keep it and read it and that one day I would read Shakespeare's plays and enjoy them.

My brothers and I thought coloured comedians with their unfamiliar vernacular and accents were the greatest. For years we kept a set of records made by a couple of coloured crosstalk comedians called Moran and Mack, the Two Black Crows. My younger brother and I knew their patter by heart. We still remember a lot of it and sometimes when we meet we go off into the routine:

"Say! Done go look at all dat black smoke coming outa dat chimly! Ah sure bet dat ol' fireman's busy!"

"Dunno 'bout busy. Everytime dere's an excursion, Ah's always broke."

"You wouldn't be broke if you worked."

"Oh, Ah'd work all right if Ah found any pleasure in it."

"*No matter 'bout pleasure; remembah it's de early bird what catches de worm . . .*"

But I remember Florence Mills best of all, with her big soft eyes, her soft voice and gentle manners. She once tipped me a pound note and on another occasion gave me a very large jigsaw puzzle. I remember how shocked my parents were when they learned of her sudden death in New York. We often used to play her records. It is a very long time ago, but I can still hear her voice singing *Silver Rose*. I recall the melody and snatches of the verse.

> *Silver, silver, silver rose,*
> *How I wonder where she goes,*
> *God above knows how I love her,*
> *Silver, silver rose . . .*

Florence Mills was called "the girl with the silver voice." She was, indeed, the silver rose.

Above. The author's father standing behind a playbill caricature of Florence Mills.

Below. The author's father with two performers from *Blackbirds*. The man on the right is Johnny Hudgins.

The first edition of Lew Leslie's *Blackbirds* in 1926, with its all-star cast of coloured talent, proved a huge success in England and in 1927 a second edition opened at the London Pavilion. Again the show was a hit. It featured many items which had appeared in the first show as well as several new acts and original sketches.

The humour of the cross-talk comedians, Williams and Taylor, the slick dancing of the Three Eddies all dressed in grey bowlers, grey jackets, checked trousers and wearing white spectacles, and the inimitable silences of Johnny Hudgins, particularly his silent sketch of a man skating, caused loud applause. The pace and spectacle of the revue excited everyone, but it was for the star of the show, Florence Mills, that the special acclaim was reserved.

Her slick appearance, her own brand of singing and dancing captivated nightly audiences and the press raved about her. The Prince of Wales came to see her many times and this provoked rumours and much speculation. Florence Mills had been the star of several revues in New York before coming to Europe. Her *Dixie to Broadway* in 1925 had been a resounding success. When she appeared in Britain the famous, the famed, the noted and the notorious all came to see her and were enraptured when she sang, *I can't give you anything but love*. When she died a year or two later, Constant Lambert wrote an Elegaic Blues piece in her memory.

Florence Mills once explained how she had evolved her particular brand of singing. She said that when she had been a child her mother often sang negro spirituals and how, whenever there had been a violent storm, with thunder and lightning, Florence had sat watching her mother rocking to and fro crooning to herself, not because she felt frightened but because she found it soothed the tension. The frightened

The two comedians, Williams and Taylor, in their chop suey routine.

Right. Florence Mills as she appeared in the second edition of *Blackbirds*.

Florence listened and was comforted. Florence said that in later years, when she went way down South to do a show, she remembered the old songs of her mother and when she was doing a number with another girl she started to croon the tune in just the way her mother had done.

This crooning quality, displayed by many negro singers of the time, was inbred—a hidden rhythm, a syncopation that extended to their every movement, every gesture, every facial expression. It hinted at a melancholy, a quiet sadness that even the liveliest jazz rhythm could not entirely dissipate.

At the age of four Florence Mills had appeared on the stage in Washington. She had subsequently played in cabarets to white audiences slumming in Harlem. She deplored the role of coloured people in the contemporary American scene. She had prospered, but the attitude of too many Americans to their coloured compatriots saddened her, as did the condition of negroes in the Southern states. But Florence felt sure attitudes were gradually changing and would change considerably. She knew they had to. She said that the negro was creative, artistic and inventive, with much to offer the world, let alone American society.

Today, by any standards, Florence Mills with her talents and sparkling personality, her sensitivity and charm, would be judged as outstanding; in the vernacular of today, a beautiful person, never to be forgotten by anybody who had met her or had seen her performances on the stage.

9

*1926 will be a
ROVER year!*

Why not own the car "hall-marked" by the Royal Automobile Club?

The sterling merits of the 14/45 h.p. Rover have been "hall-marked" by the Royal Automobile Club, who have awarded it the Dewar Trophy for making the *most meritorious* performance in an R.A.C. Certified Trial during the past year. Few cars have achieved this honour—it is conferred only for the successful accomplishment of a test far beyond the capabilities of a car of mediocre quality. And the 14/45 h.p. Rover has done that—has emerged triumphant from a gruelling mountaineering trial that no car has ever before completed. This test demonstrated indisputably the really outstanding merit of the engine, chassis and four-wheel brakes of the 14/45 h.p. Rover : proved its quality beyond all question. Why not *own* this "hall-marked" car ?— we will gladly send full particulars and demonstrate the car to you *on the road*. Prices from £550.

**Sturdy as an
old sea-rover**

ROVER

THE ROVER CO. LTD.,
61, New Bond St., W.1.
Works : COVENTRY

10

Wheels within wheels

WHEN I WAS A KID ONE OF MY FRIENDS TOLD ME HIS FATHER WAS a motor-dealer in East Ham. In those days that was big stuff. I was not sure where East Ham was, but it sounded impressive. We used to go around spotting car radiators and manufacturers' badges. That was in the days before train and aeroplane spotting. I collected a set of cigarette cards of radiators and badges and considered myself pretty knowledgeable but, of course, my friend Guy, whose father was the car dealer, was considered by one and all to be the expert.

We scorned the Fords, reputed to be the cheapest of all cars, and referred to them as "tin lizzies". We used to chant a little ditty:

If you can't afford a Ford,
You nick a Unic.

Many of the taxicabs in those days were Unics.

One day Guy proudly told me his father had, indeed, just been nicked for nicking a car, and he and his brother were moving to Plaistow. So my closest contact with cars was broken for a long time. I never saw Guy again and nobody else in our street owned a car. However we all derived vicarious pleasure by following the exploits of racing drivers and we were familiar with Parry Thomas, Henry Segrave, Malcolm Campbell and John Cobb. And was not band-leader Billy Cotton a Brooklands racing driver? I remember with the boys' magazine *The Modern Boy*, there were free gifts of authentically coloured metal cut-outs of record-breaking racing cars, which we prized highly. I remember my father talking about Count Louis Zborowski who, in 1921, raced monster cars powered by aero engines, which he called "Chitty-Bang-Bangs." For many years my father had only to mention "Chitty-Bang-Bang" and my brothers and I would fall about. The Count was killed in 1924 driving a Mercedes in the Monza Grand Prix. Parry Thomas in a Higham Special broke several records at Pendine Sands in 1926 but, trying to beat his own world speed record in 1927, a chain broke and he was killed.

However the only rides in motors we used to get, other than on the buses, was by jumping on the tail-boards of lorries; that was if they did

The car of the year, 1926 version. Rover set the fashion with prices from £550, not cheap by any standards.

11

not carry a van-boy. I did once have a ride to a funeral in a Daimler, which I did not like very much, and two rides to weddings which I liked less. I heard a lot about the Rolls-Royce—we boys always used to say as a "clincher" when arguing about cars, "You can't beat a Rolls-Royce." Then there was nothing more to say. It was to be a long time before I actually examined one at close quarters, and I have never actually got around to buying one—not even a secondhand one.

Henry Ford was never a popular figure in Britain during the twenties, although his cars sold well, being about the cheapest one could buy. It was remembered that in 1915 he had chartered a "peace ship" which took him and a number of individuals with similar views to Europe in a farcical attempt to persuade belligerent governments to call off the war and that he had, in fact, made huge war profits. He had, however, handed back nearly thirty million dollars to his government, much to the astonishment of many people.

Although Henry Ford paid his workers well, he was a reactionary. He would not tolerate trade unionism in his works and he operated a scheme of petty restrictions such as forbidding his employees to smoke, not allowing them to chat while working, spying on them and seeing that their treks to the toilets were minimal. He had in 1919 endowed a newspaper, a weekly journal, which was at first anti-Semitic, but he later directed that such a policy should cease and made a public apology to the Jews who, after all, bought cars like other people.

Nevertheless, he was a philanthropist and in 1919 he erected the Henry Ford Hospital in Detroit at a cost of 7,500,000 dollars. He encouraged thrift and he had a variety of interests which included politics, collecting early Americana and folk-dancing. By many, he was considered to be as cranky as his cars.

Captain Campbell's Bluebird sinks in quicksands after a run on the Pendine Sands.

Henry Ford, controversial motor pioneer whose Model T clattered along highways all over the world.

By constantly cutting the prices of his Model T, Ford sales continued to rise but Henry Ford was slow when it came to innovations like the conventional gear shift, hydraulic brakes and self-starters. Also his cars were always black, although it was said they did range from dark to light black. Under pressure from General Motors with their "Chevvy" in the cheaper range of cars, Ford brought out his Model A and this car, for a while, captured the market. It appealed to women with whom the Model T had never been popular.

From 1920, the sale of Morris cars moved steadily forward in the field of the family car, in the face of heavy competition from Ford and Austin and by 1925, forty per cent of all cars manufactured in Britain were made by Morris despite Ford's new British patent. The bull-nosed Morris, so called because of its distinctive radiator, was perhaps the greatest car of the decade and anyone who had one was considered to be "up and coming."

When William Morris had started his works at Cowley, near Oxford, the odds against him were great. There were shortages of raw materials, skilled labour and capital and before long he was nearly bankrupted because of the slowness in the sales of his Oxford and Cowley cars. However, by cutting production costs and making penny-wise savings, with an efficient production line, he was able to announce big price reductions for his products in 1922. He increased his production fifteen-fold; his sales soared and he wiped out his debts.

13

ROLLS-ROYCE
THE BEST CAR IN THE WORLD

AN EXPERT OPINION

concerning the

NEW 20 H.P. *ROLLS-ROYCE.*

"A CAR that in performance is wholly satisfactory. It is everything that a motorist can want. It gives him motoring with a high degree of refinement, and its simplicity of construction will delight the driver whether he be owner or otherwise."

Manchester Guardian, 8 6 23.

ROLLS - ROYCE, LIMITED

Telegrams:
"Rolhead, Pccy,
London."

15, Conduit Street,
London - W.I.

Telephone:
Mayfair 6040
(4 lines).

Rolls-Royce, advertised as the best car in the world in 1923, still makes the same claim.

He had found it irksome, too, to be dependent on his suppliers and he bought them up one after the other until he had under his control engine manufacturing, body-building and carburettor production. By 1923 William Morris was offering a choice of nineteen different styles of body on the Cowley-Morris chassis as well as a variety of colours.

He flew the Union Jack above his Cowley works and he had for a slogan: "Even if you don't buy a Morris, buy a car made in Britain." Did he include British-made Fords in this category? In 1928 he launched the famous Morris Minor, a family car at the low price of between £125 and £135.

Having made a huge fortune, Morris became a philanthropist, giving considerable sums to various charitable organisations and was, of course, duly rewarded with a knighthood. The Nuffield College of Oxford and the Nuffield Foundation mark his memory.

Sir Herbert Austin, who had been knighted for having made his fortune manufacturing guns and aircraft in World War I, launched what was perhaps the first really satisfactory family car at his works near Birmingham in 1922. This was the Austin Seven. It was a four-seater, weighed less than seven cwt., could do sixty miles to the gallon and sold for £165, which was £20 cheaper than the Model T Ford. The Austin Seven made motoring possible for thousands of families for the first time and for the next sixteen years maintained its popularity, although it was the smallest car on the market. It was an Austin Seven that won the Junior Car Club's production car race in the 750 c.c. class in 1926.

Other firms produced cars selling for less than £200. There was the Singer Junior, Triumph Seven, Clyno, Standard Nine and, of course, the Morris Minor.

In the twenties the only place in England where motor racing was legal was the track at Brooklands. Because of this lack of facilities for testing racing cars, British drivers and teams were greatly handicapped but, all the same, British cars competed in the French Grand Prix and other continental racing car events with a good deal of success.

In 1923 the British Sunbeam team gained a sweeping victory in the Grand Prix held near Tours. There were sixteen starters representing France, Italy and England and the race was over a course of 497 miles. Only five cars finished the gruelling race and three out of the five were Sunbeams. The winner was Major Segrave, averaging a speed of seventy-five miles per hour. Later he was to break the world land speed record and was knighted. It is interesting to note that at the Danish speed trials, held a little earlier than that memorable Grand Prix, a Captain Campbell in a four hundred and fifty horse-power Sunbeam covered a mile at the then phenomenal speed of one hundred and forty-six miles per hour. He too was later to break the world land speed record and he became Sir Malcolm Campbell.

Above. Captain Campbell reaches a speed of 135 m.p.h. on the Pendine Sands.

The 200 m.p.h. car built for Major H. O. Segrave at Sunbeam Works, Wolverhampton.

CITROËN

THE CAR THAT CROSSED THE SAHARA

The **7.5** h.p. 2-seater

£195

The Citroën Engineers have reproduced, in this 7·5 h.p. Model, the design and qualities which have brought world-wide fame to the 11·4 h.p. Citroën, the type used for crossing the Sahara.

Built on the lines of a big car

4 Cylinders, Water-cooled.
Back Axle with differential.
Electric Lighting & Starting.
5 Michelin Wheels & Tyres.
Magneto Ignition.
Tax £8 per annum.

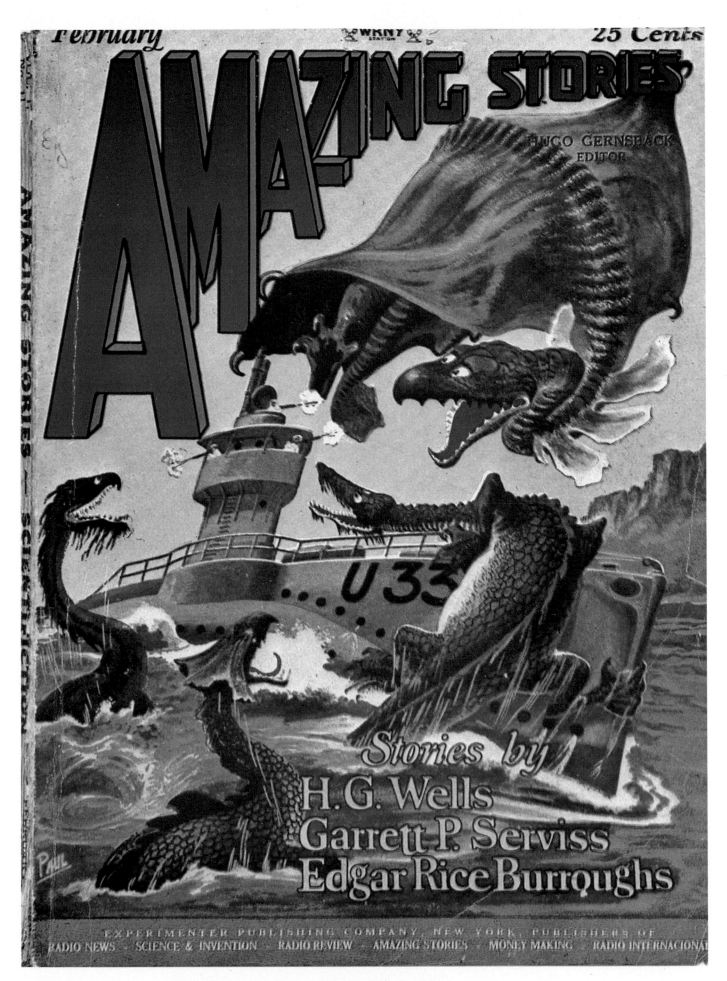

Two authors who were very popular in the 1920s,
and remain popular today, were featured on the
cover of *Amazing Stories* in February, 1927—
H. G. Wells and Edgar Rice Burroughs.

Science Wonder Stories for October, 1929 shows the
future to be just like the 1920s, style-wise, but
even more so!

Reds under the beds

I N NINETEEN-TWENTY, NOT LONG AFTER BEING DEMOBBED FROM THE army, my mother's youngest brother, who had fought in France from the age of sixteen, lost a leg in a cycle accident. After years in hospital he came to live with us and was bed-ridden for a long time before a series of operations on his hip enabled him to sit up and walk about on crutches.

He read a lot and wrote a lot. I used to read his periodicals. There was *T. P. O'Connor's* and *Cassell's Weekly*, literary magazines, *John Bull*, and on Sunday, the *Sunday Worker*. My uncle used to talk a lot about Russia, the Zinoviev letter fraud, the General Strike, the Sacco and Vanzetti case and the Arcos raid.

I soon became familiar with the old "Reds under the beds" scares, and somehow, even as a kid, these scares seemed unreal to me, sounding more like the fiction of William Le Queux and Anthony Hope, whose novels I bought on the Mile End Waste for a penny. However, in the old East End of London, it was not the "Reds under the beds" that scared the inhabitants. The real Red menace that immediately concerned them was the problem.

Everyone who lived in the East End was familiar with the Red Menace, and how difficult it was to get rid of the Red invader that came creeping out of the walls of the homes in summer. It was hard to get rid of bed bugs. It was not the Reds under the beds that scared East Enders. They had more to fear from Reds *in* the beds.

Since the Russian Revolution of 1916, rousing Reds from under the beds has been a popular pastime. In the nineteen-twenties, the British Press was strident in denouncing Russia and the Bolshevik menace, never missing an opportunity to seize hold of any potentially anti-Red item—and Red meant Labour as well as Communist—embellish it, blow it up into larger than life size, and blast away. When there was a dearth of useable material of home invention, anti-Red items were being

Looking somewhat like a kiddy car, the durable 1924 Citroen.

17

Zinoviev in 1924. Three years after the Red Letter fraud he was expelled from the Communist Party. He was shot in 1936.

spawned all the time and developed into monsters in the U.S.A. They were all grist for the British paper-mill.

The Red hand was seen at work everywhere; strikes, bombs, riots in India, fighting in China, spies and, of course, the Labour Party and the Trade Unions were riddled with Reds working with one aim—to start a bloody revolution. The Reds were a menace to the establishment; the establishment controlled the mass media; the media were used to control the masses. That meant men, women and children.

Children are susceptible to propaganda. Opinions and prejudices formed at an early age often continue through a lifetime, especially if nurtured along the way. In the early twenties the daily strip cartoon in the *Daily Mirror*, Pip, Squeak and Wilfred, often featured a villainous, bearded Russian Bolshevik with a smoking black spherical bomb in his hand and his equally villainous moustachioed Bolshevik dog, Popski, in attendance.

Russian villains abounded in the boys' papers along with the yellow peril. Perhaps it was just a fashion, a convenience for writers and artists rather than a reflection of prejudice or a means of propaganda. Perhaps it was the policy of the newspaper proprietors who published most of the blood and thunders of the period. But, as far as anti-Red news items were concerned, they were produced in deadly earnest for a set purpose; to discredit, to influence, to brainwash.

On October 25, 1924, the week before the General Election, the *Dail Mail* published a letter which was purported to have been written by the Russian Commissar, Zinoviev, in which he gave instructions to British Communists to infiltrate the armed forces, paralyse industry and

18

prepare for civil war. Despite the letter's contemptuous references to the British Labour Party, the *Daily Mail* announced that Ramsay MacDonald, the Labour Prime Minister, planned to lend money to Russia and increase Russian trade, allowing thousands of Russian agitators to pour into the country.

Not satisfied with publishing a photograph of Zinoviev which would show him just as a man with tousled hair, they published a drawing, a travesty, with not even a cartoon resemblance, of Zinoviev; not even a clever caricature, but a cartoon parody of a Jew such as the Jew-baiter Julius Streicher published in his yellow rag *Die Stürmer*. The *Daily Mail* claimed that Zinoviev's real name was Apfelbaum, an irrelevancy except it was to show that, as well as being a Red, he was also a Jew and that made him a double dyed villain. The British electorate was urged to vote Conservative and save Britain from the Red Menace. The letter, dated September 15, 1924, was addressed to "A. MacManus, British Representative of the Internationale," and was signed "Zinoviev, Dictator of Petrograd."

The letter was palpably a forgery, but it was good enough to hoodwink the masses. The Conservatives were home and dry. Later it was said that Ramsay MacDonald had known of the letter for two weeks and it was he who had, indeed, sent copies to the Foreign Office. It was not until the newspapers had published the story that the Foreign Office hurriedly published details together with the draft of a strong protest to the Soviet Government. The Foreign Office claimed that publication of the letter had been delayed until the authenticity of the letter had been proven, but Zinoviev denied that he had written the letter and denounced it as a forgery. The Soviet Government demanded an apology from Britain, but the Foreign Office who had, in fact, had a copy of the letter in their possession since October 10, repeated that they were quite satisfied the letter was genuine. If they were, they as well as the British public were being fooled.

The General Strike was called at midnight on May 3, 1926, in support of the coal miners. The miners were being squeezed by the coal owners who had been given back control of the mines and had immediately put the clock back by reverting to the pre-war system of paying the miners which, of course, meant a reduction in the already low rates of pay as well as longer working hours.

As usual, the strike was seen by the Press as being against the public interests and the work of the Reds. One of the first actions of the strikers, which had precipitated the strike, had been the refusal of *Daily Mail* printers to produce an edition of the paper containing a scurrilous leading article saying that the strike was "a revolutionary movement intended to inflict suffering upon the great mass of innocent persons in the community."

But who were the strikers and their families if they were not the mass of people? The strikers knew they were not revolutionaries; they knew,

Frame from the famous *Daily Mirror* strip—Pip, Squeak and Wilfred.

too, that when newspapers referred to public interests and public opinion, the newspapers meant the interests and opinions of the newspaper proprietors, the establishment and the real "I'm all right Jacks" of the middle class.

Soon all the newspapers were hit by the strike. Then, on May 5, the *British Gazette*, published by His Majesty's Stationery Office and edited by Winston Churchill, made its appearance. It was of two pages and was the only paper except for a single sheet published by the *Daily Express* and printed and distributed by blacklegs and strike-breakers; and the *British Worker*, produced by strikers badly handicapped by lack of printing ink and paper and means of distribution.

The *British Gazette* claimed it was the answer to the "Strike Makers' Plans to Paralyse Public Opinion." One of the headlines was "Communist Leader Arrested."

Saklatvala, the Communist M.P., had been arrested on May 3 on a warrant charging him with inciting the public to cause a breach of the peace during a speech he had made in Hyde Park on May Day. A detective sergeant, giving evidence in court, claimed to have taken shorthand notes of Saklatvala's speech. The piece read out in court and quoted in the *British Gazette* was reminiscent of the Zinoviev letter of 1924. In any case, worse things had been said in worse crises by all sorts of people in Hyde Park, but once again it was a time to drag out Reds from under the beds.

In May 1927, Sir Wyndham Borlax Childs, head of the Special Branch of the C.I.D., directed police raids on the London headquarters of Arcos, the Russian Trading company, in Moorgate. It was said by the Foreign Office that the company was a front for subversive activity and that documents that had disappeared from the War Office would be found there. Hundreds of police were involved and in a few hours offices were ransacked and safes broken open with oxy-acetylene burners. Papers and documents were confiscated but none of the missing War Office documents was found. If other evidence of Russian espionage was found it was not made public. However, diplomatic relations with Russia were broken off and officials of Arcos sent back to Russia.

Government newspaper, the *British Gazette*, published during the General Strike.

PLEASE PASS ON THIS COPY OR DISPLAY IT

The British Gazette

Published by His Majesty's Stationery Office.

| No. 6 | LONDON, TUESDAY, MAY 11, 1926. | ONE PENNY. |

SUPPLIES IMPROVING EVERYWHERE.	"DIRECT ACTION."	THE FIASCO AT OSTEND.	LINER SAILINGS UNAFFECTED.	THE TRUTH of the COAL NEGOTIATIONS
MOST SUCCESSFUL DAY SINCE THE STRIKE BEGAN.	Sir H. Slesser's Significant Opinion. A Socialist Admission.	Story Of Miners' Failure.	30 Vessels Discharging at Liverpool.	Where the Responsibility Rests
STILL MORE TRAINS:	"There has recently arisen for consideration the question how far a strike called for political objects—" direct action," as the journalists have called it—that is, a strike to interfere with or constrain the Government in conduct which the trade unions do not approve, can be said to be a strike in contemplation or furtherance of a trade dispute. This matter has fortunately not yet	SEVERE SNUB FOR MR. HODGES. Partial Embargo.	SOUTHAMPTON DOCKS NORMAL. Reports from Liverpool and Southampton indicate that the trade of these ports is practically normal. Ships are arriving and	CONSTITUTIONAL GOVERNMENT CHALLENGED

20

Above. A story from a New York newspaper of October 1929, illustrating the antics of American Red-baiters.

On November 16, 1928, two men, McCartney and Hansen, were arrested and charged with spying for the Russians. MI5 had been alerted in April and McCartney had been put under surveillance. Hansen, thought to be the organiser of the spy ring, was a student and a German national, but McCartney, who came from a wealthy family, was an Englishman. Only these two men were arrested although McCartney testified that three more men, a test pilot, a Tank Regiment sergeant and an officer in the Special Branch, were involved.

The prosecution conceded that the spies had had knowledge of the projected Arcos raid which suggested that the story of a confederate in Special Branch was true, but no more arrests were made. Sir Wyndham Borlax Childs, however, resigned unexpectedly the same month as the spy trial took place.

The trial brought out accounts of secret meetings, the usual handing over of duff information, the usual recognition signals between spies—the carrying of a red book under the arm—and the statement that McCartney had joined the Communist Party in April, a month before the Arcos raid. It was said he had immediately been assigned the important job of contact man in Hansen's organisation by the Russians; had immediately hooked a potential informant named Markland who had immediately thought to go and see Admiral Sir Reginald Hall, chief of Naval Intelligence, who had immediately passed Markland on to MI5 where a senior officer, Peter Hamilton, was immediately put in charge of the case and who immediately used Markland to bait the spies. All this had happened in one month, according to MI5.

Who then was this convenient Communist spy, McCartney? Twenty-nine years old at the time of his arrest, Wilfred Thomas McCartney had been at school in America where his father had sent him to finish his schooling. When the war broke out in 1914, at the age of sixteen, he had returned to fight in France where he had been wounded. He had been commissioned, served on the staff in Cairo, was for a short time the Governor of a Greek island, had been a King's Messenger between Cairo and Rome, then had gone back to fight in France. He was taken prisoner, but succeeded in making a daring escape. And all this before he was twenty.

He later inherited a fortune from his father, dissipated it in having a good time, was convicted for drunken brawling and imprisoned for attempted burglary. Finally he became a spy. Whatever he was or called himself, McCartney certainly was no Communist. However, soon after the trial MI5 adopted the practice of planting their agents in the Communist Party and subsequently in other parties, too.

In America, Red scares were ever present in the nineteen-twenties. Reds were seen everywhere. All Russians were suspect, including stars of opera, ballet and theatre. Some Hollywood stars came under suspicion of being Communists years before the McCarthy era. In September 1920, when the offices of John Pierpont Morgan, the American multi-millionaire banker, were bombed and many people were killed and injured, who but the Reds were guilty? What about Sacco and Vanzetti?

On April 15, 1920 in South Braintree, Mass., Parmenter, paymaster of a shoe factory and Berardelli, his bodyguard, were shot dead by bandits who escaped with £3,750. Witnesses stated that the crime had been committed by four men using a large black automobile. Such a vehicle was found abandoned some distance from the scene of the crime and tracks from a smaller automobile were found nearby. The police reasoned that the smaller automobile must have been used by the crooks to continue their getaway. A garage owner in West Bridgewater, ten miles from South Braintree, said that on May 5, four men had called at his garage for a small automobile owned by one of them. Two of the men were traced on the same day and arrested on a streetcar. They were Nicola Sacco, a shoemaker, and Bartolomeo Vanzetti, a fish pedlar. It was alleged that both men were carrying pistols, and a pamphlet announcing an anti-capitalist meeting at which Vanzetti was to speak was found in Sacco's pocket. It was also alleged that Vanzetti was carrying several 12 gauge shotgun shells at the time of his arrest.

In an unsuccessful payroll robbery attempt at Bridgewater on December 24, 1919 a 12 gauge shotgun had been used. Vanzetti was tried for the robbery on this and other flimsy evidence and despite an alibi sworn by thirty witnesses was convicted and sentenced to a prison term of twelve to fifteen years.

Subsequently both men were tried for the Braintree murders before Judge Thayer in July 1921. There were ninety-nine witnesses for the defence whose evidence would show that the two defendants could not possibly have been present in Braintree at the time of the murders, but they were found guilty before a biased judge who had referred to them as "dago anarchistic bastards." They were sentenced to death.

World reaction to the travesty of a trial was violent and the fight to get a new trial for the two men began. But despite new evidence in the men's favour the case dragged on and on until November 1925 when Celestino Madeiros, a gangster convicted of another murder, confessed that he had taken part in the South Braintree robbery. He said he had been one of a gang led by Joe Morelli that had been responsible for the crime and that neither Sacco or Vanzetti had been involved, but on October 24, 1926 Judge Thayer denied the petition based on the confession and ignored allegations of federal activity against the defendants which had been taking place secretly even prior to their arrest.

From all over the world came protests against the injustices of the trial but an independent committee set up in America to study the case concluded that, in its opinion, the defendants had received a fair trial and there was legally no case for clemency; this despite the publication of a review of the case by Professor Felix Frankfurter of Harvard University shortly before, in which he exonerated Sacco and Vanzetti.

There were successive stays of execution and Sacco went on a hunger

Sacco and Vanzetti in handcuffs; two scapegoats who died in the electric chair in 1927.

strike for thirty days. There were demonstrations in favour of the unfortunate men in Stockholm, Rome and Paris. Bombs were exploded in two New York subways and in a church in Philadelphia as well as at the house of one of the trial jurors, the Mayor of Baltimore. The day before the execution date 200,000 people rallied at a mass protest in Hyde Park and the next day the police charged another Hyde Park meeting. But all in vain.

On August 23, 1927, just over six years after their arrest, Sacco and Vanzetti were put to death in the electric chair. And from the chair Vanzetti still protested his innocence.

Yet during the period between the National Prohibition Act coming into force in the U.S.A. on January 17, 1920 and the time of the execution of Sacco and Vanzetti in 1927, compatriots of theirs like Al Capone, Johnny Torrio, the Gennas, and dozens of others like them, had flouted the law, corrupted politicians, judges, police and members of the public, shooting and bombing openly and practically daily, and had got away with it.

The Mob, not the Reds, ruled Chicago; the Mob, not the Reds, were running New York. It was not the Reds who were corrupting the American nation wholesale. It was the Mob. And how many people really cared? Certainly none of those who were getting what they wanted, what the gangsters were supplying—booze, gambling, whores and bribes—and they included a lot of people, many of them in high places. And after all, what had Sacco and Vanzetti done for them?

Is there something fishy about Reds under the beds? There is. They're usually red herrings.

23

What Price Glory

I WENT TO SEE *WHAT PRICE GLORY* AT THE OLD MILE END EMPIRE, formerly called the Paragon. Years later I saw another version of the film, featuring James Cagney as Captain Flagg and Dan Dailey as Sergeant Quirt, but although James Cagney was one of my favourites the film did not have the same magic for me as did the first version which, when I saw it again on a much later occasion, still seemed to have some of that same old magic that had thrilled me so many years before.

A novelty in the original film was the blowing of a raspberry by an actor-soldier and the effect on youngsters who saw the film was devastating. Thereafter they blew raspberries at all and sundry at the slightest provocation and often without provocation. Sometimes a youngster would preface a raspberry by shouting, "What Price Glory." At school, I was given the "stick" by the headmaster, six cuts on the palm of each hand, for giving the raspberry to the science master, and I was not the only pupil to suffer punishment for such an offence. At a special school assembly we were warned of dire consequences if we did not cease "the disgusting practice." But threats were unavailing. The raspberry had come to stay.

For some years Friday night at the Mile End Empire was gala night. In addition to the usual main film, a second feature, a couple of talkie "shorts", a cartoon film and a newsreel, there was also a stage show of eight amateurs turns. The cinema would be packed. Every seat in the house, in the pit, the circle and the gallery, the "gods", would be taken, with people standing in the aisles and along the barriers which lined the sides and the back of the pit. Outside the cinema, besides the vendors of penny bags of roasted peanuts and halfpenny bags of popcorn, there was a man who used to appear on Friday nights only.

This man sold a small article which cost a penny. It consisted of a wooden tube about the size of a cigarette, with two thin rubber flaps fixed at one end. By blowing through the tube the flaps would be caused to vibrate, resulting in the loudest and most satisfactory raspberry any youngster could ever hope to blow. The instrument was called simply, a "farter."

Above. A spectacular war scene; the advance from a sunken road.

Below left. After the action. American troops behind the lines.

Below right. American soldiers crouch in a hollow waiting for a night attack.

There we would sit, cosy in the cinema on gala night, waiting for the turns to come on, with our blowers at the ready. We used to allow each act about thirty seconds to please us and if it did not we used to give the act the "bird" with raspberries from every corner of the house. It was cruel, no doubt, but at least we did give an act what we thought was a fair chance. Female sopranos, unfunny comedians, paper tearers and farmyard impressionists were our chief victims.

At other times, during a love scene in some dreary film, usually British in those days, the effect of a solitary raspberry, blown with superb timing at the moment of a passionate kiss or when some sequence had reached a boring climax, was shattering, and those of the audience who had not already walked out would roar with laughter and feel some satisfaction for having suffered in silence.

One thing is for certain. *What Price Glory* certainly made its mark at the Mile End Empire.

25

Ex-boxer Victor McLaglen, who played Captain Flagg, served in the British Army in World War I.

Below. Captain Flagg chats with Charmaine during a spell behind the lines.

Seven years after the end of World War I there was a rush of war films each intended to be more lavish and penetrating than its predecessor. *Havoc* with George O'Brien and Madge Bellamy; *Madamoiselle from Armentieres* with John Stewart and Estelle Brody; *The Big Parade* with John Gilbert and Renée Adorée, and documentaries and semi-documentaries. *Coronel and Falkland Islands*, *Ypres*, *Mons* and *The Somme*, all appeared between 1925 and 1927.

Members of the public were ready to view the war objectively and to recall what, to most of them, was the biggest, most sustained and harrowing series of events they had ever experienced in one way or another. Despite the lingering memory of the war in all its horror, it seemed the time to bring forth the legend and the romance.

Each last war had been a landmark as a rich source of legend and romance for writers and artists, with its heroes, and enemy as ready-made villains. Waterloo was the great inspiration for years until Crimea; then had come the Boer Wars to replace them in legend until 1914–18.

The Great War surpassed all previous wars in its magnitude and sheer horror and Britain was still in a state of shock for many years after it ended. Then had come reaction and nostalgia and with it the flood of books based on personal experience, the inquests, the quest for explanations and the seeking out of scapegoats. Then followed the war films providing vicarious thrills for those who remembered the times but had not experienced the trenches and an object of curiosity for those who had.

What Price Glory, the war film which made a sensational arrival at the old Plaza in the Haymarket in 1927, was a close adaptation of a play by Lawrence Stallings and Maxwell Anderson, which had been presented in New York with the bent-nosed Louis Wolheim playing the part of Captain Flagg. Louis Wolheim was later to play the memorable Katt in that most famous of all war movies, the screen adaptation of Erich Remarque's *All Quiet on the Western Front*, with Lew Ayres.

Lawrence Stallings drew on his own experiences with the U.S. Marines in France in 1918 for his story. For a long time after the war had ended, he was still in hospital recovering from the effects of a leg amputation. He wrote *The Big Parade* which, under the direction of Raoul Walsh, had been a great success as a movie in 1925 and it took several years of hard slogging to shape *What Price Glory* into a super movie.

It did not have the realism of *All Quiet*, nor its intriguing delineation of character. It failed to show the true squalor, the degradation, the boredom and waste of war as did *All Quiet*. It lacked its haunting quality and uncompromising condemnation of war. There was too much of the contrived situation and slapstick in *What Price Glory*.

Victor McLaglen as Captain Flagg, and the immaculate Edmund Lowe as Sergeant Quirt, were hardly convincing except as a sort of comic knock-about double act. Their rivalry for the favours of the inn-keeper's daughter, Charmaine, played by Dolores del Rio, provided some sort of plot although, by present day audiences, Charmaine would probably be regarded as a bit of a drag. Flagg and Quirt seemed to regard her as really nothing more than a sort of "poker-chippy" to be won in a game—certainly not as a prize to be won in the matrimonial stakes. As for the most unlikely relationship between Captain and Sergeant, ex-servicemen watching their antics in the movie, must have viewed them with a good deal of cynicism.

Ted McNamara, Sammy Cohen and L. Lewisohn provided the humour in the ranks which, of course, had to feature Irish, Jewish and other representatives of the great American melting-pot, although it was not thought necessary in those days to include any negroes. Pathos was introduced by the tear-jerking episode of a dear mother's-boy dying in action and if it were hammy, nobody probably noticed it at the time. However, the movie left no doubt about the Americans winning the war.

Nevertheless, there was much realism in the spectacular battle scenes and some contrived realism in the way actors, playing the part of soldiers, seemed to be mouthing real swear-words on occasions; the movie was, of course, a "silent." It was the first time the "raspberry" was featured on the screen. Ted McNamara mouthed it; the effects man in the orchestra-pit, with beautiful timing, gave it life and sound. That, and the song called *Charmaine*, which came out at the same time as the movie, captured the public imagination and lasted longer in memory, generally, than the film itself.

Fashion foibles

A YEAR OR SO BEFORE THE LAST WAR BROKE OUT I HAD STARTED drawing fashion sketches and before long, I was having success in selling them to dress and mantle manufacturers in London's East and West End. At that time sketches and fashion books came mostly from Paris, Vienna and New York and were usually punted around by pretty girls. Most of the cutter-designers who bought sketches were males.

I used to wade through fashion books of the twenties and thirties looking for inspiration, but most of my ideas for designs and their presentation came from the continental sketches. I had not been taught fashion drawing at art school. Dress and mantle sketches usually sold for 2s. 6d. to 3s. 6d. each and as far as I was concerned seemed easier to sketch than sell.

The first time I took out a folio of sketches to show to a fashion designer-cutter was one evening and I walked into the manufacturers cold. I was more than a little apprehensive for in those days I was extremely shy of meeting people and lacked confidence in just about everything I did. However, I asked to see the designer and my first surprise was to find it was a woman and that she would see me; my second surprise was when she selected a dozen sketches; my third surprise when I was paid on the spot and left thirty shillings richer.

I immediately called for a girl friend, told her what, and off we went to the West End where she helped me blow the money.

In the twenties the hemlines of dresses went up and down, up and down and up and down again. Breasts appeared and disappeared. Waistlines crept backwards and forwards along the torso from below the bust to below the hips and sometimes vanished completely. A woman's draped body often seemed shapeless and her appearance in a bathing suit, more often than not, confirmed this.

The true designers of women's fashions of the twenties were based on

Left. Marshall and Snelgrove's sale features cami-knickers; very trendy in 1927.

Right. Debenham and Freebody bargains, including a leather coat for less than £6.

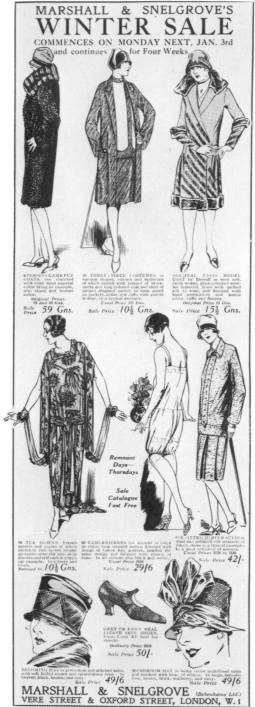

Paris where the influence on current trends emanated from such internationally known fashion houses as those of Captain Edward Molyneux, Coco Chanel, Patou, Lucien Lelong and Schiaperelli. Manufacturers employed beady-eyed sketchers to attend fashion shows to pirate the new styles. This was a form of industrial espionage that flourished in the period.

Yet for a time fashion was a prerogotive of the more well off and in

Aquascutum garments of 1923, devised in the best interests of the sportswoman. Prices were in the region of £10.

general there was scarcely any basic difference in the styles worn by girls of fifteen and women of fifty. As for the mere male, fashions changed almost imperceptibly and in appearance a boy of fifteen was more or less a sawed-off version of his father.

The most outstanding event of male fashion was in 1925 when Oxford bags arrived, when trousers flapped around the knees and ankles like wide split skirts. In 1924 musical comedy star Jack Buchanan had introduced the double-breasted dinner jacket which, of course, was no great shakes to the man in the street who considered himself lucky if he possessed a suit for Sunday, bought off the peg at the Fifty Shilling Tailors. And plus fours, an exaggerated version of knickerbockers, which also made their appearance at the time were all right for a minority who played golf and flashy men about town and country with other suits in their wardrobes. However, clothes for women in general were beginning to take on a new look. Factories for the mass production of dresses and coats, using new fabrics and textiles like bouclé, printed art crepes, marocains and chiffons, were bringing attractive garments within the price range of the girls working in shops,

The time-honoured sailor theme; another version of the sailor hat. And the hat with the vagabond crown.

offices and showrooms. Even copies of Paris models were to be had at reasonable prices.

Sadly, there were no nylon stockings on the market, but good legs looked good legs in silk, artificial silk and even cotton lisle. Sometimes in the latter part of the twenties a male observer of the female form could get a quick flash of pink flesh, when bloomers had gradually crept up the thighs away from stocking tops to become cami knickers and French knickers, and garters had given way to suspenders. Only ballet dancers wore tights.

Most men and women wore hats. Men's hats had changed little over the years, but as usual women's hats varied continually from the sublime to the ridiculous and fashion writers gushed their way through the twenties in the wake of everchanging styles to describe them. Quoted here are two blurbs by the same writer, the first written in July 1923 . . .

"No woman at this date in the calendar considers she is equipped for the holidays unless she is in the possession of a felt hat from Henry Heath's, 105–109 Oxford Street. Two of his latest triumphs find pictorial expression on this page. It will be remembered that this firm is responsible for the celebrated Sans Souci which in the very finest fur felt is 29/6. It can be adapted to any shape and will roll up quite flat for travelling."

The second in January 1927 . . . "Women always become enthusiastic about Henry Heath's Knightsbridge hats for country wear, three of which find pictorial expression in this page. As will be seen, one model has a crown of the vagabond persuasion, the brim being turned down at the back; the other two are variations on the time honoured sailor theme." (Oh, my hat! Tiddly winks old man, suck a lemon if you can.) "A few words must be said about the absolutely waterproof velvet berets for 37/6. They are very close fitting with a narrow brim." Few words indeed. Phew!

With regards to women's hair styles a report on a lecture by a hair stylist in 1926 just about sums up the picture. The hair stylist, Monsieur Gaston Boudon of the firm of Emilé of London and Paris, gave his lecture illustrated by lantern slides. He expressed his opinion that the then-fashionable shingle would last for another two years. This pronouncement apparently knocked the women off their seats. Monsieur Gaston went on to say it was exaggeration that killed fashion, explaining that in hair styling as well as in everything else, evolution was important. He showed slides to illustrate that this was so in ancient times as well as in modern times. The women were enthralled by this remarkable revelation. Monsieur Gaston reminded them that the shingle had been preceded by the bobtail, a shorter version of the bob; then had come the Eton crop which was shorter still. This had been followed by the Hindenburg, a very close Germanic crop. Gasps from the audience. To be sure and only one step away from the Yul Brinner and Kojak which, as we know, have so far been for men only.

Nanook
and the documentary

MANY YEARS AGO, EVEN BEFORE WE HAD STARTED SCHOOL, MY mother took my brother and me to see the film *Nanook of the North*. For a while after that I would tip a kitchen chair on its back, my brother would sit on the rung and I would push him around the room. The chair was our sledge; I was Nanook. That was when I was not riding a broomstick called Tony and being Tom Mix, my greatest cowboy hero of them all. I have since seen a more modern version of *Nanook* with Anthony Quinn, but it was not the same. Somehow I could not recapture any first taste of the Frozen North and the pleasure of those first sledge rides on the kitchen chair, not even of subsequent occasions when I was someone of the Mounties driving the kitchen chair, brandishing the whip for my whipping top and shouting, "Mush!"

The original film story of Nanook, chief of the Itivimutis, a tribe of Eskimoes, was hailed by the critics at the time of its release in 1922 as one of the most enthralling pictures ever made. It was lauded for its stark realism, the starring of people who were not actors, and the novelty it brought to the screen.

Later, reviewing this type of Flaherty film, John Grierson, a Scottish film-maker, used the word "documentary" to describe it and the type of films he was producing. The name, documentary, stuck.

By 1921, film cameras had covered locations in the wild and glamorous West, the sun drenched and glamorous South and the mysterious and sinister East, but the Arctic regions of the North had been left out in the cold, so to speak. By and large the Arctic was not the sort of location that would lure ordinary film-makers, actors and actresses. They did not have to trek to the Tundra to make films requiring Arctic backgrounds, and the effects men could always be relied on to produce flurries of cotton wool snow when required.

But Robert J. Flaherty was seeking authenticity when he adopted the

THE MAY 1927

Picturegoer

MONTHLY

Vol. 13
Nº 77

1/-net

FREE—inside
"Coming Fashions" Paper
Pattern of Dainty
Tennis Frock

The Picturegoer in 1927 depicts Victor McLaglen in
What Price Glory.

Amazing Stories, an American science-fiction
magazine dated August, 1927. The story
illustrated was *The War of the Worlds* by H. G.
Wells. Nine years after WW1, and eleven years
before WW11 . . .

Left. Nyla, Nanook's wife, bears the Eskimo's burden and looks happy about it.

Right. A young Eskimo surveys a world of a billion ice lollies.

Below. Eskimo fishermen hauling their boat ashore.

expedient of trekking across the Arctic snow and ice with a minimum of filming equipment. He cast the characters for his film as he discovered them, 800 miles north of civilisation's outposts in the walrus and seal hunting grounds, fishing grounds and in the igloo villages of the Eskimoes. There, Flaherty, with a limited vocabulary of the Eskimo language, contrived to live and work with the Eskimoes through 1920 and 1921, amusing them on occasions with his gramophone records, to

33

Left. Nanook preparing to harpoon a seal.

Eskimo fishermen hauling their boat ashore.

make his unique film. Every character appearing in *Nanook of the North* was an Eskimo recruited from the small Utivimutis tribe, inhabiting the Ungava Peninsular, then one of the most remote areas in the North.

Nanook, the star of the film, and Nyla, his wife, who was also his leading lady, and their three children were allowed to go, more or less, about their normal tasks as far as possible, in front of the film cameras. This original approach and use of the natural backdrop of snow and ice resulted in the classic realism that has since become the mark of the documentary film.

Nanook was the first real deviation from the conventional type of screenplay. It contrasted the harsh starkness of the North with the simplicity of a patient, hardworking, primitively equipped people. It showed them struggling for survival in the bleakness of an uncompromising climate. It demonstrated that, in spite of hardships, the Eskimo is kind, cheerful, tolerant and good tempered. It cast a light on a way of life almost inconceivable to moviegoers of the period.

Here were the fur-swathed inhabitants of another planet, hunting for food in freezing deserts practically devoid of any vegetation. Lashed by stinging snow, haunted by blizzards they toiled in a sun starved world. Here were people huddled in primitive shelters, extracting from life the pleasure of family. Here were uncomplaining people making every minute of their lives count. Here were the heroes of the North where all too often nature could be the villain in his bitterest moods. Here was real life drama played out in the freezing wastes. Here was novelty for moviegoers sitting back in their comfortable plush chairs in a warm cinema and having their first glimpse of a people so different from themselves. They had no doubt that they were looking at the real thing. *Nanook of the North* had arrived and so had the documentary.

The Manassa Mauler

MY FATHER WAS A BOXING FAN AND USED TO GO TO THE FIGHTS at the Premierland, the old Wonderland. He called us down from bed in the middle of the night to hear the radio running commentary on the Joe Louis–Tommy Farr fight from America in 1937. Of all fighters, Jack Dempsey was his idol. He talked about him a lot and practically gave us a blow by blow account from time to time, of the Dempsey–Carpentier fight. I became interested in boxing myself while at school and later fought as a featherweight. I always wished I were at least thirty pounds heavier. Years later when I was, the extra pounds were not all that welcome after all.

In 1944, while serving in South-east Asia, I met Jack Dempsey when, as a Lieutenant-Commander in the U.S. Coastguard, he was on a public relations tour of the area. About ten years ago in New York, I went to his restaurant on Broadway, not far from Times Square, with an American friend. I mentioned to Dempsey that I had met him before during the war and he was delighted, and so were we by his genuine friendliness and strong personality. He insisted our dinner was on the house.

A few years ago I was staying in Paris with my wife and one morning, as we were having coffee at a sidewalk café on the corner of the Boulevard des Capucines and Rue Caumartin, she drew my attention to a tall, smartly dressed, very distinguished gentleman across the street waiting to cross. He held two very large dogs on leash. We both recognised him. It was Georges Carpentier. I had to talk to him and I did. He was most charming and said he was surprised that we had recognised him. Of course he was as well-known as Dempsey, especially in France where he had appeared in films, on the stage, on the radio and later on television. We chatted a while about the fight game and I mentioned the occasions I had met Jack Dempsey and recalled his fight with the champion. Carpentier smiled ruefully and said he thought I was too young to remember that one. It had, indeed, taken place fifty years previously but I thought, as I looked at Georges Carpentier, he looked fit enought to go a few rounds with anybody.

It was sad to learn that the splendid warrior passed away just a few

35

weeks before writing this. I have met many boxers over the years but I am glad of the coincidences that led me to meet two of the greatest.

The outstanding sporting figure of the twenties was without a doubt, Jack Dempsey, one of the most colourful fighters of the age who, even until this day is still remembered as the idol of them all. Born in Manassa, Colorado, in June 1895, his real name was William Harrison Dempsey and he began his boxing career at seventeen in western mining camps, entering the professional arena two years later. It was when he met the great Jack Kearns in 1917 that Dempsey's future started to change rapidly and in 1919 he smashed his way to a spectacular victory over giant Jesse Willard to win the world heavyweight crown in three unforgettable rounds.

By 1920 Dempsey was the idol of the world, his fame spreading like wildfire even though radio and television had not yet arrived. Of course, there was plenty of "ballyhoo." Doc Kearns was a past master in publicity and promotion and he steered Dempsey along to bigger and bigger "gates." Dempsey, defending his title on September 6, 1920, stopped Billy Miske, a tough boxer he had already beaten twice before, in three rounds in Michigan and knocked out the redoubtable Bill Brennan in the twelfth round in Madison Square Garden in December 1920.

Then, on July 2, 1921, Tex Rickard, one of the most famous of all promoters, staged the bout often referred to as "the Battle of the Century," in a place called Boyle's Thirty Acres in New Jersey, between Jack Dempsey and France's pride and joy, the "Orchid Kid", "Gorgeous" Georges Carpentier.

Although only a light-heavyweight, Carpentier's speed, accuracy and deadly right hand were thought to be formidable weapons against the tiger ferocity of the "Manassa Mauler" as Jack was called. The bout was a huge financial success for Rickard and an exciting four rounds for the huge crowd that turned out for what was boxing's first million-dollar extravaganza. Just about every well-known personality in the world of sport, movies, stage, theatre and politics must have been present at the fight.

Jack won the first round easily enough, but in the second, "Gorgeous" Georges went into the attack, rocking the champion back on his heels. However, Georges had had his moment for out came Jack for the third round with wicked intent. A smash to the stomach and a storm of vicious body blows soon had the Frenchman helpless in a corner. Only the bell saved him.

The end came early in the next round. A stunning left hook from the champion to the body of the challenger dropped him for a count of nine.

Opposite. The greatest heavyweight champion of them all; Dempsey in peak condition.

36

Jack listens to his director on a film set in Hollywood.

Tough Angel Firpo who knocked Dempsey out of the ring.

Below. Dempsey in a characteristic pose.

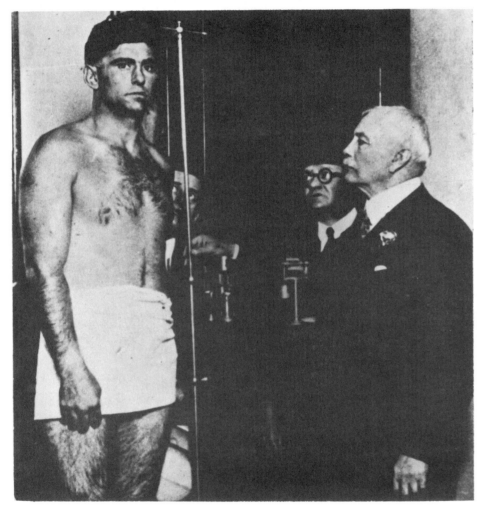

Argentinian Luis Angel Firpo, known as "the Wild Bull of the Pampas," at the Polo Grounds in New York. The fight lasted less than two rounds but it was a thrilling whirl of dramatic action.

In the first round Dempsey sent the lumbering challenger sprawling to the canvas seven times. Battered, bloody and reeling, Firpo came back full of fight. He floored Dempsey twice and then sent him flying through the ropes. The crowd roared. If ringsiders had not pushed Jack back into the ring he must have failed to beat the count and Firpo

Opposite top. Dempsey–
Carpentier fight; Dempsey has
the challenger in all sorts of
trouble.

Opposite below. Carpentier takes
the full count in round four.

would have captured the heavyweight crown there and then.

But Firpo, with the prize within his grasp as the champion swayed groggily in front of him, was unable to seize his great opportunity and in the second round a fully recovered, seething Dempsey swiftly demolished his dangerous opponent. Firpo was slammed to the canvas twice, the second time with a short-arm right to the jaw for the full count. Had one of Firpo's handlers remained calm enough when Dempsey had been sent hurtling through the ropes and had been helped back into the ring in contravention of the rules, to claim that Dempsey had been out for ten seconds, Gallagher, the referee, would have found himself with as hot a potato as he had ever had to handle in his career. But none of Firpo's men ever made such a claim at the time and it was bad luck for Firpo. All the same, only a true champion with the heart and fighting ability of Dempsey could have got back into the ring after the bruising, bewildering experience of being knocked through the ropes, to destroy such a rugged opponent as Firpo in a matter of a few minutes.

In 1925 the New York State Athletic Commission insisted that Dempsey fight Harry Wills, the negro challenger for the title, but Jack turned down the match and was consequently barred from fighting in the Empire State. The Boxing Board appealed to Tex Rickard but he said that New York governor, Al Smith, had hinted that a negro–white bout was not desirable in New York. However, this report was vehemently denied by James A. Farley, chairman of the New York Commission. There were plenty of recriminations and much behind the scenes activity and when Rickard arranged a fight between Dempsey and Gene Tunney for the Yankee Stadium the Commission was having none of it and refused to sanction the bout. So the promotion went to the Sesquicentennial Stadium, Philadelphia.

The contest took place in September 1926 with a gate of nearly two million dollars and the biggest attendance in boxing history. The fight was in drenching rain which soaked the crowd and contestants and made the canvas slippery and treacherous. Tunney was in far better physical condition than was Dempsey, who was in a depressed state which the weather did not help. Dempsey had broken with his manager after marriage to movie star Estelle Taylor and his matrimonial affairs were not too happy at that time.

The champion seemed sluggish and detached; he lacked his usual tearaway bustle. His style was awkward and Tunney tied him up and made him look amateurish. Dempsey seemed to have lost his deadly sting and savage intensity.

In contrast, Tunney was sharp and skilful, cool and calculating. He beat Jack to the punch and was more accurate with his shots. In the fifth round Dempsey sustained a cut eye and gradually was worn down, seeming to lose heart, and was quite unable to rally in the way he had so often done before. The younger man won the ten-round contest on points comfortably and the disconsolate ex-champion finished the fight

41

Top. Dempsey is outpointed by his younger challenger, Gene Tunney, in September 1926.

Below. Dempsey stands poised for victory, but Tunney, after the famous "long count", came back to win a points victory.

with a fat eye, a bruised face, a pair of wobbly knees and a severely damaged ego.

But it was not long before Dempsey was back looking for a return contest with Gene Tunney. However, it was first necessary for Rickard to restore the image of the invincible "Mauler" and rebuild the public confidence, so rudely shaken by their idol's clearcut defeat by the ex-Marine. The next opponent selected for Dempsey was Jack Sharkey, the ex-sailor, a boxer with a good record, including a win over that same formidable Harry Wills who had vainly challenged Jack for the championship.

The fight took place in July 1927 at the Yankee Stadium, New York, and again there was a million dollar gate. The bout started with the faster Sharkey leaving a dazed Dempsey slumped on his stool after the first round. Had Sharkey elected to continue to fight as he had been instructed, at long range and scoring points over his opponent, the result might have been different. However, somehow he thought to change his cautious approach and entered into a slugging match with the scowling ex-champion. In this he was no match for the tough battler, Jack Dempsey. Dempsey pounded the luckless Sharkey with a fusillade of savage body blows that caused him to wince and lose ground. Then, in the seventh round, Dempsey crowded the ex-sailor with a flurry of body blows, one or two low by accident in the swift action, rather than by design, but none of them in the least damaging. Then followed a swift punch to Sharkey's stomach at close quarters. This took all the fight out of Sharkey. Grimacing with pain, he unwisely turned to the referee to protest he had been struck by a low blow, instead of first dropping to one knee. It was not in Dempsey's nature to miss such an opportunity. He hooked a thundering thump to Sharkey's jaw, putting him away for the session. There were cries that Sharkey had been fouled. The referee hesitated. He seemed to be unsure and looked down at Sharkey. Then Bill Duffy, Dempsey's second, shouted from his corner to the referee, "Count that man, O'Sullivan. Count him!" Jack O'Sullivan glanced at McPartland, the knockdown timekeeper, and took up the count with him from six until ten. Dempsey was the victor by a knockout.

Next, Tex Rickard announced that a Dempsey–Tunney return match was fixed. On September 23, 1927 the two men met at Soldiers' Field, Chicago, for a title bout and the fifth million-dollar gate, this time the record sum of 2,685,660 dollars. This battle has become famous as "the Battle of the Long Count," and controversy over the decision has been raging ever since.

Before the fight both contestants had been told that, under the rules of boxing in the State of Illinois, even when a fighter had been floored he would not be considered to be off his feet until his opponent had gone to the neutral corner, farthest from the man on the canvas, and the referee would not start the count before he had done so.

Until the seventh round Tunney had been systematically sniping at a frustrated Dempsey. The round started with Gene landing a right to Jack's head, following this with several stiff jabs. Stung to action, Dempsey stormed his opponent's defences, landing half a dozen solid blows including two heavy rights to the head, a long sizzling left hook and a right to the jaw. Tunney toppled to the canvas close to the ropes, where he sat back in an ungainly posture, his left hand groping instinctively for the middle rope.

It looked as though Dempsey was within an ace of regaining his title. The timekeeper started to count but the referee took no notice as he moved in on Dempsey who was crouching over his stricken opponent. He urged Dempsey to go to a neutral corner. Stubbornly, Dempsey persisted in hovering close to his victim and it was not until he finally did go to a neutral corner that the referee, Dave Barry, started his count from one. The official timekeeper and many ringsiders maintained that Gene was down for fourteen seconds, while some sportswriters insisted that it was more like seventeen. It was as Barry tolled the count of nine that Tunney rose to his feet. Dempsey rushed across the length of the ring to finish him off, but the wily champion needed all the breathing space he could get and he moved away with Jack trying to catch him and calling him to come in and fight. But Tunney bobbed and weaved and even managed to crease Dempsey with a right to the stomach and they finished the round in a clinch.

In round eight Tunney, with his head cleared, danced around the ring, jabbing at the disheartened Jack, then dropped him with a swift right to the jaw. The crowd shrieked and yelled but Dempsey was up on his feet immediately. Nevertheless, he was adjudged to have lost the round and the subsequent two by a wide margin. Tunney was awarded the decision and was in fact judged by knowledgable boxing experts to have won seven of the ten rounds.

Tunney's version of the "long count" was that he was aware of the situation even as he hit the canvas and Dempsey stood over him. He was prepared to take a count of nine before getting up. He said he was watching Dave Barry, waiting for him to take up the count and that he was ready to rise at any time. But many eyewitnesses of the incident were not prepared to concede this. Photographs of Tunney, glassy-eyed on the canvas, seem to make Tunney's version debatable, yet there are other photographs taken when Dempsey had retired to a neutral corner which show Tunney looking alertly across the ring at him, still clutching that middle rope and indeed looking as if waiting to rise to his feet.

Dave Barry said that as Tunney hit the canvas his eyes were glazed and it was apparent he had been badly hurt, yet he said that his impression was that Tunney had regained his senses in three or four seconds and that, even if Dempsey had retired to a neutral corner immediately, Tunney would have been able to rise in good shape before the final count.

44

Horse racing enthusiast and racehorse owner, Jack poses with a young jockey.

Some months later in New York, speaking of the memorable fight at Soldiers' Field, Dempsey said, "I am not within forty per cent of the man I used to be. I learned that in the seventh round in Chicago. There I had Tunney out but instead of taking it calmly and getting the title back I hung around, not going to my corner for some seconds. Then, when Tunney finally got up, I found the reaction on me was greater than it had been on Tunney. I found that I was weak. I had allowed the excitement to get the better of me. My eyes haven't been as good as they should be. If I read for a while they get tired. I find if I stay up late, I feel it the next day."

That fight at Soldiers' Field was really the end of the Dempsey era and the end of the glamour of the heavyweight title for a long while. He did try to make a comeback and he went on to make a fortune in boxing exhibitions. But he was a man of many interests and the ring gave way to other activities. For a while he operated the Dempsey-Vanderbilt Hotel in Miami and, of course, his restaurant in Manhattan became world renowned and a venue for the famous in every sphere of entertainment. The glamour of Jack Dempsey, the Manassa Mauler lives on. To many he is still the "Champ."

45

The terrible Turks

IN THE EARLY TWENTIES, WHEN OUR FAMILY WAS LIVING IN BRIGHTON, I heard a good deal about the "Terrible Turks." An aunt of mine by marriage had a brother who had been taken prisoner-of-war by the Turks in the Siege of Kut in Mesopotamia, now Iraq. He had eventually been repatriated, but due to ill-treatment in a prisoner-of-war camp, where he had received a severe rifle butt-stroke across the head from a Turkish guard, his mental health deteriorated. He was to spend the next fifty years of his life in a mental institution.

Two of my uncles had fought against the Turks in the Allenby Campaign in Palestine and the younger of the two had been in the army of occupation in Constantinople for a short time after the war; I still have the revolver holster he gave me as a war souvenir. I always remember my uncles saying that the Turks were good soldiers. As a child I never thought of them as being anything else but soldiers.

The first time I came into contact with Turkish people was in Cyprus a few years ago when I visited the Turkish section of Famagusta and at a small pavement cafe I got into conversation with a Turkish national from Izmir. He told me that his grandfather had been in the Turkish Army in Gallipoli when the Allies had stormed ashore in the bloody landing of 1915 and that he himself had fought in Korea under the auspices of the United Nations in 1951. I casually asked him what his father had been doing between 1939 and 1945; Turkey had remained neutral almost to the end of the war before joining the victorious allies and then taken no part in the fighting.

He grinned and said his father had been a waiter in an Istanbul hotel. For some reason it crossed my mind that "they also serve who only stand and wait."

The 11th Battalion, Royal Marines, arriving at Portsmouth from Turkey after the Treaty of Lausanne.

On July 24, 1923 after eight months of tough negotiations the definitive peace treaty between Greece, the allies and Turkey was signed at Lausanne, Switzerland. At the time it was said, echoing what

Turks fly flags in
Constantinople to celebrate
the British evacuation.

had been said of the Treaty of Amiens in 1802, that it was a peace which everybody was glad of and nobody was proud of. However it did put an end to the uneasy conditions of the armed watchfulness of the British, almost as irksome in some respects as overt hostilities, and enabled the Government to bring home the 15,000 troops occupying the Straits.

Nevertheless, there was general uneasiness about the terms of the treaty which had restored to Turkey, defeated in the 1914–18 war, 11,000 square miles of European territory which had remained to her after the Balkan War of 1912–13. There was a good deal of scepticism about elaborate arrangements that had been made to demilitarise the Straits and Turkey's European frontier, as no means had been made for enforcing them. Furthermore all allied claims to reparations had been renounced.

The most unsatisfactory feature of the Treaty, according to opinion at the time, was that the allies had agreed to the arrangements for the compulsory exchange of populations whereby a purely national Turkish state would be created and thousands of Armenians and Greeks would find themselves at the mercy of the Turks, as would all foreigners resident in Turkey as well as European institutions, churches and businesses.

However, under Kemal Pasha, the Turkish "strong man" who had defended the Straits against the allies in World War I, Turkey was to take great strides into the present from the middle ages, although somehow Turkey always managed to lag a stride or two behind the rest of Europe.

With the defeat of the Turks in 1918 and the complete disintegration of their Empire, the allies had occupied Constantinople, but a Turkish National Assembly was set up in Angora in Asia Minor. A strong Turkish army influenced by Mustapha Kemal had taken the field and the allies authorised the Greeks to advance in the face of the Turkish threat. The Turks had retreated, but in 1921 they won significant victories against the Greeks and now the allies were quick to find plenty of excuses for not supporting their Greek protegé. The fall of President Venizelos in Greece and the return of King Constantine, whom the allies distrusted, was one excuse and the Greeks found themselves out on a limb. They went it alone and were branded the aggressors.

With so many millions of Moslems within their empires and occupied territories, neither the British or the French wanted to embroil themselves in hostilities against the country. They had traditionally bolstered it as a bulwark against Russian expansion, despite the fact that Turkey had turned against them to help Germany in every possible way in 1914. But in 1922, when Mustapha Kemal smashed the Greeks and sent them reeling back to the coast of Asia Minor into the sea, and seemed set to advance on into the neutral zone, this was more than the British had bargained for. It seemed for a dangerous while that Britain

48

H. H. Harris' advertising poster for Bovril in 1923
was to become a national institution.

A stark statement of fact. *Choc-Full of Goodness!*
Produced for the Nestlé company in 1928 by an
anonymous graphics artist.

British troops loading the *Hecuba*, the first transport to leave for home during the evacuation.

Left. Sir Charles Harington, Allied C-in-C in Turkey, with an A.D.C.

Right. Ismet Pasha, Turkish peace envoy, returns to Constantinople.

would find herself at war with Turkey, not a happy thought for the British people so soon after the holocaust of 1914–18. The French and Italians had opted out. However, the British commander, General Harrington, and Mustapha Kemal, now expediently deemed to be a wise statesman by the British, arranged an armistice.

Nevertheless, the net result was that although Turkey lost Egypt, Syria, Palestine, Mesopotamia, her Arabian possessions, Cyprus and the Dodecanese she maintained her foothold in Europe and there it stays, firmly planted.

49

50

Look—no actors!

MY MOTHER TELLS ME THAT THE FIRST CARTOON FILMS I EVER SAW were based on Aesop's fables and I remember them only vaguely. Later I saw Felix the Cat cartoons which achieved world-wide popularity. There was a song called *Felix Kept on Walking*, and we used to play the record on the gramophone so frequently that it became scratched and cracked and it finally finished up in pieces when my father accidentally sat on it. I recall the tune and some of the words:

> Once there was a little cat
> With a tummy nice and fat,
> And he had a name;
> Felix was his name.

Anybody who had a black cat at that time called it Felix and I believe the name is still popular with cat lovers to this day. I know at home, over the years, one Felix succeeded another. One of our cats called Felix unexpectedly turned out to be a female and she had a litter of three kittens which we kept. When we called, "Felix," all four cats used to come running.

I saw Disney's *Oswald the Rabbit* and subsequently Mickey Mouse, which soon became a fixture in the cinema. Children felt cheated if they went to a matinée and there was no cartoon film on the programme.

During World War II I met a number of American servicemen in South-east Asia, members of a special photo unit, who had worked as artists and animators for Disney Studios in Hollywood. Several of them had later worked on service instruction cartoon films before coming out to the Far East. One of them told me that before he had got a job with Disney, he had been employed by a firm manufacturing pesticides where for several years he had drawn nothing but mice, rats, beetles and other pests for catalogues and advertisements. To amuse himself he had drawn comic strips featuring these pests, one of which he had entitled Louis the Louse.

Not long after the war a film unit was set up in Cookham by David Hand to produce British cartoon features. Two of my former colleagues, Bob Monkhouse of television fame, and Maurice Saporito, a Fleet

Street artist, often used to talk of those days when they had worked in Cookham and the difficulties that had been encountered in trying to make the project viable.

For my part, I have been a fan of Sylvester and Tweetie Pie ever since one day in my office I heard writer and broadcaster Denis Gifford singing, "I taught I taw a puddy tat." He sang it quite well, I thought.

In 1922 Paul Terry brought to the screen the fables of Aesop as animated cartoon comedy features, and these were received with a good deal of acclaim and commentary by film critics and the public at large. One writer suggested that had Aesop himself been alive at the time, he would probably have been able to write wittier sub-titles for the films, although he did think that the humour that had been introduced into the series was irresistible.

The presentation of each cartoon film represented a colossal amount of hard labour, thousands of separate pictures having to be drawn by the artist, then laboriously photographed. Every movement, no matter how slight, of hands, arms, feet, mouth and eyes meant that a series of pictures had to be drawn to represent the movement for the cameras.

Of course, the pioneers of this form of motion picture had to construct their action slowly by hand and it took weeks to prepare a ten-minute film. There was a lot of trial and error in creating pictorial characters for the Aesop series, yet the results were remarkably good.

Frames from Terry's *Aesop's Fables*. Left to right: *The Hare and Frogs, The Lion and the Mouse, The Wolf and the Kid*, and *The Conceited Donkey*.

Aesop's Fables, produced by Grangers, were pretentiously described at the time as sugar-coated pills of wisdom, the wisdom being reflected by rundown photography of each cartoon character in the fable and then adding an updated version. The fundamental truths of the patriarchal hunchback of Phrygia, recounted in the Court of Croesus, were as pertinent to the screen as they had ever been, and appealed to young and old. Children laughed at the antics of the grotesque screen characters, adults enjoyed the antics and professed to appreciate the underlying significance, no matter how trite, as their excuse for watching. Terry's films included *The Mice at War*, *The Hare and the Frogs*, *The Conceited Donkey*, *The Lion and the Mouse* and *The Wolf and the Kid*, and they appeared in many cinemas at weekly intervals.

Paul Terry, whose skill was in creating droll animals and extracting humour from their mannerisms, said he realised the humorous possibilities of animals in a curious way. He was watching a film consisting of a series of camera studies showing the effect of music on various animals at the London Zoo. Their reactions and grimaces caused roars of laughter from the audience and it occurred to Terry that animals had natural screen personalities and were a rich mine of humour.

All it required was for him to exaggerate the idiosyncracies and mannerisms of the animals with facile pencil studies, and these observations provided him with the material for use in cartoon animation. He then created a new form of humour by endowing an animal with a human sense of the ridiculous. The combination of a precocious mouse armed with a saw severing the bonds of a ludicrous lion seated in human fashion, or a goat dancing on its hind legs to the tune played on a

53

whistle by a leering wolf, presented animals aping humans in a way that appealed to adults as well as children. It was soon obvious that the animated cartoon film was a film with a future.

In 1923, at the age of twenty-two, Walt Disney established his own studio for the production of motion pictures. His first venture was to make *Alice in Cartoonland*, featuring a live actress playing the part of Alice, combined with animated cartoon figures. Disney followed this with *Oswald the Rabbit*, his first complete animated cartoon feature without live actors.

In 1928 he began production on the first series of Mickey Mouse pictures. Then came the talkies and Disney held back the Mickey Mouse series so the new sound synchronisation could be incorporated. His first Mickey Mouse movie with sound was released in September 1928 and it was an immediate success. At the time Disney was employing a staff of twenty-five, but then a new company, Disney Enterprises, was formed to exploit the character appearing in the films, marketing and licensing comic books, books, strip cartoons and toys. Characters originally created for Mickey Mouse now appeared in feature films of their own, particularly Donald Duck, Pluto the Pup and Goofy.

Disney's *Silly Symphonies* were a series of films where the sound track was used with new effectiveness. The first of these, appearing in 1929, was *Skeleton Dance*, which featured Saint-Saens' *Danse Macabre*. The unusual combination of comic animation with a theme of classical music proved highly successful.

Felix the Cat was originated by an Australian, Pat Sullivan, but the character was never supported by personality characters in the way Mickey Mouse was, nor were the multiple exploitation possibilities.

Felix the Cat, who arrived in Britain in 1923, is seen here faced with the German inflation situation.

The civilised anthropophagi

SOME YEARS AGO, IN THE FIFTIES, I WAS MOTORING DOWN THROUGH Germany with my wife and son, on the way to Innsbruck in Austria. Due to a carburettor fault we stopped over for a few days at Lindau, a small resort town on Lake Constance. It was our first visit to Germany and, despite the wonderful scenery, I found it depressing, especially the drive through the Black Forest where, had I seen were-wolves it would not have surprised me.

The hotel where we stayed was luxurious, comfortable and efficiently run; the town was pleasant, clean and picturesque, but somehow everything seemed unreal. I found the people with whom we had to deal detached, aloof and often downright arrogant, and it was difficult to make any real contact, although there was little language difficulty. But our chambermaid was different.

She was plump, pleasant, smiling and spoke English. She was in her early fifties and looked a good deal younger. Her husband had been taken prisoner in North Africa by the British during the war and had died a few years after his return to Germany in an accident at work.

She had lived in Düsseldorf before her marriage and told us about her life there as a child and in her early teens; about hard times, un-employment, street fights and later the wicked war. She then mentioned that she had lived in Mettmännerstrasse in Düsseldorf, adding, "That's the street where Peter Kurten lived—the one who killed all those people." I told her I remembered reading about Kurten in the English papers while I was still at school. She said she had known Kurten, not to talk to, but by sight and that, looking back, he reminded her some-what of Adolf Hitler, adding quickly, *"Gott hab' ihm selig!"* I was not sure to whom she was referring with her pious, "God rest his soul," but either way I found it chilling.

There was an inn in the town centre where we had lunch one day. The inn sign I found strange for a Bavarian town. It was a large wrought iron Star of David in a circle with a beer stein in the centre, suspended from a beautiful bracket outside the inn. As I photographed it I wond-ered if it had been there during the Hitler period. A few years ago I read a travel article in a London daily. It was about holidays in Bavaria

55

and featured a photograph of that inn sign at Lindau, but there was a difference; the sign had been sawn off at the edges so that it was no longer recognisable as a Star of David. What had happened to cause the change to have been made? I was never able to find out. Perhaps it happened in the new wave of anti-Semitism that swept Germany in 1959. I wonder if that pleasant, plump chambermaid noticed anything?

Choked with the stench of some three million German war-dead and black with the bitterness of defeat in World War I, the aftermath for Germany as she lurched despairingly into the twenties was suffering and hardship. She was beset by food and clothing shortages, unemployment and galloping inflation. Yet below the surface of daily life, more terrible events were taking place. Before the end of the decade four particular instances of clandestine terror broke to the surface like boils of some fatal plague, symptomatic of the infinitely more shocking eruptions yet to come another decade later. Werewolves and cannibals had come creeping back into Germany, although few realised to what extent such creatures, spawned and thriving on the rotten carcase of German retrogression, would seize, control and infect practically the whole nation.

Mass murder took place over a long period in areas where people must have had their suspicions aroused; where circumstances of a peculiar nature must have added to suspicions, but, as with the patent vileness of the growing power of the Nazis, people preferred to ignore uncomfortable manifestations, to discount rumours and just concentrate selfishly on any immediate benefits and profits that might be brought about by circumstances, no matter how dark.

Georg Grossman was a burly man, sullen and suspicious, who repulsed any attempt by neighbours to make themselves pleasant. For eight years he lived alone in the kitchen of the owner of a top storey flat in a rundown district in Berlin. He worked as a pedlar of old clothes and, when food shortages were growing and inflation was pricing many commodities out of the market, he supplemented the income from his clothing business by illicitly selling meat without ration coupons. He also kept a small allotment near the River Spree.

Often, especially at night, his neighbours would hear loud noises and strange sounds coming from his room, which he seemed to share frequently with female acquaintances. Although there were several half-hearted complaints from neighbours from time to time, nothing was done until one evening in August 1921 when the disturbance was so sustained that the landlord called the police. When Grossman did not answer their knocking, the police forced the door open. They were horrified as they took in the scene in the kitchen. It was a butcher's

Opposite. Peter Kürten, psychiatrists' enigma and outstanding candidate for the S.S., died before his time.

56

57

The tenement in Mettmannerstrasse, Düsseldorf. The arrow indicates where Kürten lived with his wife.

slaughter-house.

On a decrepit camp bed, trussed up skilfully in the way a competent butcher prepares a carcase for cutting up, was the body of a girl, not yet cold. The police searching the room found a pot containing human fingers under the bed. It was proved by the types, shapes and condition that during the previous few weeks at least three women must have been slaughtered and dismembered in the kitchen. Many people now came forward to claim that they had often seen Grossman near his allotment, disposing of parcels in the river in suspicious circumstances.

It was soon discovered that Georg Grossman had a long police record which included offences against children, and now the police believed he was responsible for the murder of scores of women who disappeared from the Berlin streets during the war years and the years following.

The trial of Grossman was in low key. The implications of his butchery and meat business were too terrible to contemplate. A number of uneasy people took heart from the allegations by witnesses that they had seen

58

Grossman disposing of parcels in the river. Grossman was sentenced to death and the pronouncement sent him into fits of laughter as he feigned insanity.

However, he cheated the block by hanging himself in his cell. (Execution at that time in Germany was still carried out in the medieval manner, by beheading with an axe wielded by an executioner wearing a high top-hat.)

In 1928, the River Leine running through Hanover was dragged by the police after a number of skulls had been discovered by children playing on the river banks. Bones and skulls were dredged up from the waters and at least twenty-six skeletons were reconstructed from them. All the skeletons seemed to be of young men in their late teens or early twenties.

Police searched their missing persons' files and also the records of homosexuals, both genuine and perverted. Their routine enquiries embraced a person who was a known homosexual pervert with a long police record, but he was also a useful police spy, unofficial detective and associate of local brownshirts, the private Nazi army of the notorious pervert Roehm, whose entourage was made up of male prostitutes. The person was Fritz Haarman, a rag and bone dealer and, although police found bloodstained clothing in the attic where he lived, he was able to allay their suspicions, explaining the blood by claiming he suffered from haemorrhoids. Perhaps the police believed him because they wanted to. They found Haarman useful in their work and also were not above accepting presents from him. However, the chief of the Hanover police, in view of this close association between members of his force and Haarman, decided to send to Berlin for help and two detectives came from Berlin to watch Haarman.

Haarman had a close attachment for a surly youth named Grans whom he used to ply with presents of clothes and money. In February 1923 two female prostitute friends of Grans had happened to call at Haarman's rooms while both men were away and, snooping around, had found a large quantity of meat. In that time of acute meat shortages their suspicions were aroused and they took a sample to the police. A police expert reported that the sample was pork and the police continued to employ Haarman. In fact, soon afterwards when a former police inspector started business as a private detective he took in Haarman as a partner. In this way the clothes dealer and purveyor of meats obtained a warrant card which he used to intimidate many of his victims. At this time he was also a recruiting agent for the Black Reichswehr and was active against Communists.

Haarman had become well known in the Schieber Market—the black market in the square outside the Head Railway Station in Hanover where he did a thriving trade in *Gehamstertes Fleisch*, smuggled meat and secondhand clothing. He also assisted the railway police in the station and, in the role of detective, he waylaid hopeful young men

Below. Dummy dressed in clothes of one of Kürten's victims was used by police to help find the Düsseldorf killer.

The house in Köln Mulheim where Kürten murdered Christine Klein.

arriving late without anywhere to stay for the night. Many of them became his victims. He killed by suddenly seizing the Adam's apple of a victim between his strong teeth.

One night Haarman was seen prowling among the sleeping men in the station. Then in the early hours of the morning a sudden row broke out between him and a powerful youngster named Fromm. Haarman called to the police for help, saying he had caught a man travelling without a ticket. Fromm counter-claimed with a charge that Haarman had made indecent suggestions. The Berlin detectives, who had been keeping watch on Haarman, now interceded and rushed both the yelling men to the police station. The opportunity was taken to search Haarman's rooms thoroughly. Grans was found and was, too, taken to the police station.

Quantities of clothing and small objects found in the rooms were to become the basis of material evidence against Haarman. He explained that the clothes were his stock in trade as a secondhand clothing dealer, and the bloodstains on the walls of his rooms the results of his other business as a butcher. But, by a coincidence, a woman who had come up from the country to inquire at police headquarters about her missing son recognised that some of the clothing worn by Grans, belonged in fact to her son and identified other articles amongst the impounded clothing. The Hanover police, now under pressure, resorted to rougher tactics. Haarman, under ruthless interrogation, finally broke down and confessed his crimes but alleged that Grans had been the instigator and had also been his accomplice.

Haarman was found guilty of twenty-four murders and had surely committed many more. That he had been guilty of the piecemeal selling of his victims' bodies was never proved, nor was any great effort made to prove it. Rumours about the Ogre of Hanover were disquieting enough and nobody wished to know the truth of the matter. It was a case of "what the eyes don't see, the heart doesn't grieve for."

There were many people who must have suspected Haarman's nocturnal prowlings in the years preceding his arrest, the occasional police calls at Haarman's lodgings in their constant search for missing youths and the comings and goings of boys to the door of Haarman day and night. Haarman's reputation as a homosexual and his previous convictions for various offences were well known. Nobody questioned where he replenished his stock of meat and clothing for the Schieber Market. The noise of chopping in his rooms and his appearances on the stairway, quite openly, taking a bucket of blood covered by a towel to the backyard seemed to excite no curiosity, let alone suspicion. It seemed police and the good citizens of the town were quite prepared to ignore suspicions of murder and cannibalism until Haarman's trial. Then, for the first time, some revulsion for Haarman was shown.

Haarman was tried and sentenced to be decapitated. Grans was given imprisonment for life, but the sentence was eventually reduced. After his release from prison he disappeared for a while, but turned up some years later as a guard at Dachau where, no doubt, his experience was of great value to the authorities.

Denke, a quiet man of farming stock, lived alone on the ground floor of a house he owned in Münsterberg, where he did all his own domestic chores, much to the amusement of the local hausfraus. He was the organ-blower at the local church and, as was customary at funerals in Bavaria, he was the one who marched ahead carrying the apostolic cross. He got on well with his tenants, a coachman, Herr Gabriel, and his wife, and a schoolteacher named Voigt who had eleven children living with him.

In December 1924, hearing the sound of a violent struggle, the crashing of overturned furniture, then calls for help, Gabriel, believing that his landlord was being attacked, ran downstairs from his room above Denke's and through the open door of Denke's flat. He found Denke struggling with a young man bleeding from head wounds. The

61

youth managed to gasp before he collapsed that Denke had struck him with a pickaxe which was lying on the floor.

Denke was arrested and his flat searched. The police found the identity papers of a dozen journeymen apprentices and a sack of assorted clothing. Then came the nauseating revelation of the full horror of the so-ordinary Münsterberg house. The large kitchen cupboard contained two tubs of meat pickled in brine, two large pots of rendered-down fat and a chest full of bones, while in a shed in the backyard the police found several basins of salted meat.

Little imagination was needed to realise what kind of meat was stocked in Denke's storehouse. The flesh visibly bore characteristics of male as well as female humans. The most staggering discovery was a ledger in which entries had been carefully made of the name, weight and date of pickling of each carcase. On checking the dates the police found they more or less tallied with dates on which certain missing persons had last been seen, and these extended from 1921 to 1924. The missing persons included travelling journeymen, men and women beggars and tramps.

These poor people had come to beg at Denke's door and had served to stock his shop. Yet, despite the fact that there were thirteen people living in his house and that he had often been seen carrying pans of meat and buckets of blood from his kitchen to his shed, Denke had gone about his business for years undisturbed. If there were many people buying meat from Denke who had had their suspicions, it seemed they had preferred to shrug off any uneasiness and pretend to themselves

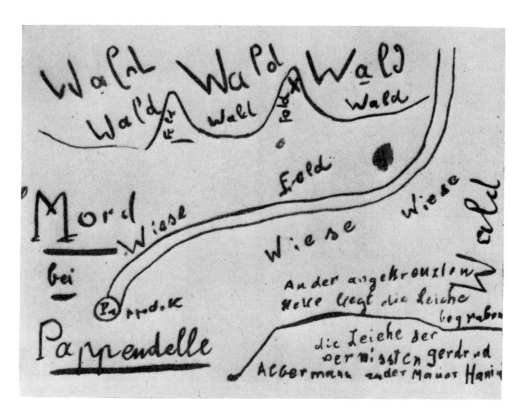

Sketch map made by Kürten in a letter he sent to police, indicating where the body of Gertrude Albermann could be found.

Above. A sign of the times. Nazis waiting to surrender after their abortive putsch in 1923. Himmler carries the white flag.

that nothing was amiss. Times were hard and there were other things to worry about; one had to be practical.

Denke had nothing to say on the subject. He was a quiet man; just a hardworking German waiting for Götterdämmerung. At least he did not deal in frivolities such as lampshades made from human skin as did some of his compatriots at a later date. A few days after his arrest Denke hanged himself by his braces.

"I must own . . . I really always was in a frame of mind when I had the desire—or perhaps you will say, the urge—to kill somebody. The more people the better. Yes, if I had the means of doing so I would have killed whole masses of people—brought about catastrophes." So spoke Peter Kurten, the monster of Düsseldorf, to the psychiatrist, Professor Berg, while in prison.

Had Kurten lived it is possible that under Hitler he would have realised his ambitions. Even this inspired killer could not have imagined in his wildest flights of fancy the "night of the long knives" and the Nazis' mass murders of World War II.

Peter Kurten's criminal activities took place over a very long period of years and he spent a lot of his early life in prison, but he sailed through the whole of the twenties assaulting his victims, committing arson and murder until in 1929 he went on the rampage, stalking his victims, stabbing, strangling, battering, irrespective of age or sex, using knife, scissors or hammer, and killing nine of the twenty-three persons he attacked. In August 1929 alone he struck nine times and in the following year he violently assaulted ten more people. For the fifteen months

63

Samples of Kürten's handwriting in the old German script. *Right.* His ordinary writing. *Below.* Kürten's writing under stress. This letter to the Communist newspaper, *Freiheit*, led to his identification.

Dark eyes and red lips! A simple and compelling
Danish poster of 1925.

A poster designed for the Underground Electric
Railways Company in 1924 by F. C. Herrick. This
British design reflects magnificantly the image of
the 1920s.

before his arrest in 1930 he led the Düsseldorf police a danse macabre, baiting them by providing clues, writing them letters and even providing maps to show them where to find bodies of his victims.

While Kurten was at large the whole town of Düsseldorf was in terror. As one writer pointed out, one of the most horrible features about Kurten's nocturnal prowlings was the unavoidable analogy with the werewolf and vampire. Kurten had a predeliction for drinking the blood that gushed from the wounds of his victims.

But he was an ordinary looking man who might not draw a second glance in the street. He was fair haired and sedate looking. He was softly spoken and had a serious, gentle and trustworthy manner. Nevertheless he was forceful and singleminded, and women found him attractive. He was married and his wife resented his success with young women and was suspicious of his activities in this direction, but she had no realisation of the full nature of his crimes. Outwardly, Kurten seemed fond of children and witnesses testified that children seemed to be fond of him.

He was caught when, in a rare moment of compassion, he allowed the twenty-year-old Maria Budlick to escape his clutches. It was a mistake that led Chief Inspector Gennet to his very doorstep. Kurten had become acquainted with Maria when she had arrived from Cologne to take up a job in Düsseldorf and he had come to her assistance when she had been importuned by a stranger at the railway station. Kurten had taken the girl back to his room in Mettmännerstrasse, but after she had accepted a glass of milk and a slice of bread she insisted that she leave to find a lodging for the night. Kurten agreed to find a place for her, but lured her to Grafenberg Woods on the outskirts of the town, to a place known, strangely enough, as Wolf's Glen. He grabbed her throat and then, curiously for him, he relented. He asked her if she remembered where he lived. Fortunately she said she did not. The lie saved her life and cost Kurten his.

The girl remembered the name of the street where Kurten lived; she had seen it in the lamplight. Two plainclothesmen helped her to retrace her steps to Kurten's flat and a short while later Kurten, the Düsseldorf Monster, was under arrest.

He had actually committed his first murder in 1913 when he had killed Christina Klein, but he had attempted murder as early as 1899. He was not mad, no more than Hitler, Himmler, Heydrich and Eichmann were mad. Mass murderers are not mad as mad dogs are mad. Their crimes are part of their nature.

The Empire at Wembley

I RECENTLY WALKED AROUND THE OLD EXHIBITION GROUNDS AT Wembley. Some of the massive concrete buildings are still standing; most are crumbling. A few are being used as industrial premises; others were in use until a short while ago, but are now empty. The famous lion motif can still be seen on some of the buildings and names like Stephenson Gate and Watt Gate are still just about discernable on what remains of the great Palace of Engineering, where the girdered roof and derelict interior, strewn with chunks of concrete, gives it the appearance of some vast bombed-out railway terminus. I park my car outside this deserted building every day and go on to town by train from Wembley Park Station.

My family moved from Brighton to London in 1924 at the time of the great Empire Exhibition at Wembley, but I was never taken there, although I remember hearing a lot of talk about it; of the palaces and pavilions of eighteen dominions and colonies; the grand replicas of the Taj Mahal, an African village and old London Bridge; the massed bands and firework displays and Tex Austin's rodeo at the Stadium.

Today, only the Stadium remains to reflect the departed glory of that great Exhibition. People still throng to Wembley regularly for all sorts of sporting events, rallies and spectacles, but the rest of the exhibition buildings, like the great Empire they once represented, have crumbled away.

"This Exhibition will enable us to take stock of the resources, actual and potential, of the Empire as a whole, to consider where these exist and how they can best be developed and utilised, to take counsel together how the people can co-operate to supply one another's needs and to promote national wellbeing . . . We hope that the success of the Exhibition may bring lasting benefit not to the Empire only, but to mankind in general."

With these fine words, relayed by the B.B.C. and sent round the

King George V and Queen Mary see their "whole Empire in little," at Wembley.

View of part of the Exhibition grounds, looking toward the stadium.

world in less than one minute, King Emperor George V opened the British Empire Exhibition at Wembley on St. George's Day, April 23, 1924. Next, the Bishop of London had his say. Then, Sir Edward Elgar, Master of the King's Musick, conducted massed bands and choirs in soul-stirring renderings of *Jerusalem*, *Land of Hope and Glory* and *Soul of the World*. After all that the hundred thousand people at the opening relaxed and milled round the Exhibition grounds.

Most of the visitors had no conception of the people and lands of the Empire. Now was their chance to learn a little, see real Indians, Burmese and Nigerians, perhaps for the first time, and if it bored them there was always the forty-acre amusement park which had cost one and a half million pounds. There they could have real fun on the scenic railway, Billy Butlin's dodgem cars, water chutes, switchback and browsing around hundreds of sideshows and shops.

The Exhibition was sited right alongside the new Metropolitan Railway extension from London with its new station at Wembley Park. Rural Wembley was on the threshold of becoming a vast suburb, to be swallowed eventually as urbanisation continued. Round the Stadium, opened in 1923, there were fifteen miles of streets and paths between the various buildings and pavilions. The roads were named Anson's Way, Drake's Way, Empire Way and other such names selected by Rudyard Kipling. The main pavilions were massive fortress-like buildings bedecked with hundreds of flapping flags.

There was the Government Pavilion with its six gigantic lions, each bigger than Landseer's famous lions in Trafalgar Square, and the Palace of Engineering, then the largest concrete building in the world, covering an area actually six and a half times bigger than Trafalgar Square. Here were exhibits of the shipbuilding industry and great mechanical exhibits among which were a special railway saloon coach built for the King of Egypt, an early railway engine, the then-latest L.N.E.R. giant locomotive, a model of an armoured cruiser built for the Japanese Navy and a sixteen-inch naval gun weighing 117 tons.

The Palace of Industry featured a sanitised mock-up of a colliery complete with stabling and pit ponies which were not blind, and real coal. Visitors were taken down a shaft to the workings in a two-decked cage and returned to the surface without gathering a speck of dirt. Mining was good clean fun at Wembley. The Palace of Arts included collections of paintings, furniture, jewellery and pottery. The Indian Pavilion was a replica of the Taj Mahal and the entrance was across a courtyard where could be seen working Baluchi carpet weavers, brass beaters from Benares, and sellers of silks from Kashmir. It seemed real enough to the vast majority of visitors despite the absence of flies and cow dung and the unpleasant smells of a Chandni Chowk or Chowringhee. There were, of course, none of the familiar India cries for backsheesh.

The Canadian Pavilion contained a representation of Jasper Park,

69

After the Exhibition, the Canadian building was dismantled.

It was here that thousands of people saw the fascinating dioramas of the Canadian Pacific Railway.

complete with waterfalls, and wildlife which included bears and foxes, and there were dozens of booths representing various aspects of Canada. Real red-coated Mounties were in attendance. The Gold Coast Pavilion had massive doors carved by African students from Accra and there was a West African mud village, hygenic of course, complete with natives, one or two topless on occasions, to add to the authenticity.

The South Africa Pavilion, built in Dutch style, contained a huge model of the Karoo landscape with springbok, eland and hartebeest. South African industry was represented by exhibits of gold and diamond workings, viniculture and ostrich farming. There were relics of the Voortrekkers—their cap tent wagons and veldt skoen—but no relics of the Boer War and no apartheid yet. There was a restaurant car standing in an especially built veldt railway station, serving what was purported to be South African food for the foolhardy. The East African building containted exhibits from Sudan, Zanzibar, Tanganyika, Kenya, Nyasaland and Uganda as well as from Mauritius and the Seychelles.

The New Zealand Pavilion had on display an eighty foot long carved Maori house. It had been resurrected from a vault in South Kensington Museum where it had been for twenty-odd years. Real Maoris were on hand to highlight the display.

Ceylon featured a collection of pearl necklaces insured for a million pounds—in those days a King's ransom and not just the going rate in any kidnapping. The Burmese, too, had their exhibits and Burmese boys demonstrated how to play Chin-Ion. A Chinese street representing the Hong Kong section, had a Chinese restaurant, a novelty in Britain in 1924 and a forerunner of the thousands to come.

Visitors flocked to Wembley from near and far to see the reconstruction of the tomb of Tutankhamen, the life-size statue made in butter of the Prince of Wales in the Canadian pavilion, and the tableau in butter

70

of the famous cricketer Jack Hobbs, at the wicket, in the Australian pavilion. One of Wembley's biggest attractions was the famous Queen's Dolls' House presented to Queen Mary. The amount it cost would have been enough to build houses for dozens of Her Majesty's poorest subjects. It was said that the Dolls' House was used to raise money for charities.

The Dolls' House had taken two years to build and furnish and had engaged the efforts of leading architects, artists, craftsmen and authors. Each room, at the most not more than two foot high, was expensively furnished down to the last detail with tiny sets of cutlery and tableware, rugs, cushions and every appurtenance to be found in a palatial residence. Even the 120 books in its library were handwritten by famous authors, who included Robert Bridges, Galsworthy, Kipling, Hardy, and Conrad. Cellars were stacked with real stores in miniature; water ran from the taps and the toilets flushed. There were four bathrooms. Most houses in Britain at that time had none. The Dolls' House was an eye-opener for people in those days before the landed gentry had gone into the business of throwing open their stately homes to the public.

May 24, 1924 was Empire Day. It was celebrated at Wembley by a huge parade in the Stadium, massed bands, a procession headed by one hundred pipers, which included a drum and fife band of three hundred, and eight thousand London school children. The fashion was set for the military tattoos of the future.

People continued to stream out to Wembley, flooding from the new station at Wembley Hill and the specially built eight-platform bus station, to stroll round the beautiful gardens, to cross picturesque bridges over lakes and streams, to wander in and out of the pavilions and spend their money on the attractions at the amusement park, whirling, careering, spinning and sliding—on the caterpillar, the Derby

71

Racer, the double track mountain chute, the Jack and Jill and hundreds
of sideshows. And at night the fun continued under brilliant floodlights
which transformed the white buildings into a breathtaking magic city.

One of the spectacles presented at the Wembley Stadium aroused a
good deal of opposition and controversy right from the start. In a blaze
of publicity the versatile showman Charles B. Cochran brought over
Tex Austin and his rodeo. There were four hundred head of cattle, four
hundred horses and dozens of cowboys to provide the novel entertainment of round-ups, steer roping, bronco busting and stampedes. Animal
lovers all over the country protested.

On the first afternoon of the show 80,000 people turned up to see it.
However, during an evening performance a steer broke its leg in a
roping exhibition and had to be destroyed. Cochran and Austin were
prosecuted and appeared before a court at Wealdstone. They were
acquitted and the show continued. The rodeo, booked for two weeks
ran for three weeks, but attendances at the Exhibition were dropping
all the time and people stayed away from the rodeo. On this occasion,
Cochran was bankrupted. When in 1975 a horse broke its leg at a show
at Wembley and was shot, people seemed less squeamish. After all, beef
is for eating and, "they shoot horses, don't they?"

The Exhibition at Wembley finally closed in October 1925 and was
not a financial success. However, the Stadium was sold and became the
home of international sport and greyhound racing. The buildings on the
site became part of a trading estate and were used as offices, warehouses
and light industrial premises. Since then new office buildings and blocks
of flats have replaced many of the old buildings, but the ghosts of
Wembley are still there. Hosts of cats, left by the concessionaires when
the Exhibition closed, roamed the deserted buildings and grounds and
their feral descendants still lurk in the bushes, sun themselves on lawns
outside blocks of flats and come running to gather around the old ladies
who come daily to feed them.

General strike

IN MAY 1926 A LITTLE BOY STOOD ON GARDINER'S CORNER, THE junction of Whitechapel and Commercial Road, watching a convoy of lorries escorted by armoured cars passing along Commercial Road on the way to the docks. That little boy was me. I stood with four silent watchers wondering vaguely if there was going to be a war and what it would be like if the machine guns, sticking out of the turrets of the armoured cars, started firing. It was exciting.

A few days later, a little boy was standing outside the old Rivoli Cinema in the Whitechapel Road watching a squad of soldiers marching towards Aldgate. The little boy was me. I suppose they were a deterrent for something or other. A show of force. Even now I cannot think where they might have been going or coming from or what their purpose was.

I watched them marching by, thrilled to bits. They wore steel helmets like I had seen in pictures of the Great War. Real soldiers marching along, their iron-shod boots clinking on the stones; not men in scarlet coats but real soldiers—soldiers in khaki uniforms with puttees and cartridge pouches, bayonets in black scabbards at their sides, and slung rifles. These were English soldiers just like those who had fought at Ypres and the Somme. Not quite. Nobody cheered them. The few people who watched were silent.

Then one of the soldiers slipped and went sprawling. The people came to life. They jeered and catcalled. It did not seem right to me—jeering our own soldiers. I remember I felt uneasy. I did not like it.

Two ladies do their bit. Lady Malcolm, with frying pan, and Lady Mountbatten outside a soup kitchen in Hyde Park.

In 1926 Arthur J. Cook, the leader of the miners, cried, "Not a minute on the day, not a penny off the pay!" He asked that miners be given safety in the mines, be allowed proper compensation, fair working hours and decent living conditions. At the time the living conditions of the miners and their families were little better than that of brow-beaten coolies in the colonies.

How the miners worked. After the strike this is the purgatory they went back to for less pay and longer hours.

The British mining industry was suffering from keen competition from the continent. Traditional English markets were being captured by France, Germany and Poland because British mine-owners, milking the mine industry, had consistently refused to spend money modernising the pits and invest in new machinery, despite the recommendations of the Sankey Report of 1919.

In March 1926 a Royal Commission under Sir Herbert Samuel was appointed to report on the condition of the coal industry. It found that three-quarters of Britain's coal was being produced at a loss; the miners were paid too much and the mine-owners were taking too much profit. Nationalisation was recommended. It was revealed that the mining income of the Duke of Northumberland was £82,000 a year. The average wage of a miner was in the region of £150 a year.

But Tory Prime Minister Stanley Baldwin turned down nationalisation, ignored the mine-owners' profits and supported their claim that miners' wages be cut by 13½ per cent and that the miners work longer hours to boot to help solve the general economic problems of the country. The T.U.C. then threatened to take strike action and call out not only the miners but industrial workers, transport workers, railwaymen and printworkers, to support them.

The Government, however, had made extensive preparations to meet the challenge with a volunteer strike-breaking force, the organisation for the maintenance of supplies, the help of industrialists' facilities

74

Arthur J. Cook, the miners' leader whose passionate appeals on behalf of the miners failed to move the ruling classes.

and emergency powers to counter any moves by strikers. Standing by were troops and naval forces and thousands of special constables. Confident in their power, the Government refused to negotiate. For good measure twelve Communist leaders were arrested and clapped into prison.

The strike started at midnight on May 3, 1926 and although the T.U.C. did everything possible to ensure the maintenance of food supplies, the Government immediately called out the Army, ostensibly to keep power and communications going. But shows of force, the wholesale deployment of middle class and upper class blacklegs, strident student dilettantes and dilettante students, were all used to intimidate the miserably depressed strikers. There was to be no pity, no concession, no mercy for them. The strike had to be broken and the miners stamped back underground.

For many of those who volunteered to do the jobs of the strikers it was an exhilarating experience. Driving buses, trains, trams and lorries was a "lark", with the attitude, "I always wanted to drive a train." So rich undergraduates and public schoolboys drove trains and buses and, as special constables, dressed in topees and jodhpurs, they sat their horses and carried long batons as if preparing to play a few chukkas of jolly old polo instead of standing by ready to crack a skull or two or knock the brains out of some hungry striker.

Hundreds of drivers and other volunteers were housed and fed at

75

Above. Milk churns piled up on the Embankment to impress the public with a bogus threat to food supplies.

Armoured cars in London streets to symbolise civil unrest.

Opposite. Another way to impress the public: a police guard on a bus and a useless single strand of barbed wire to simulate a martial atmosphere.

76

Hardship for miners; fun for some. Girls hitch a ride to work.

Right. A hopeful cyclist wonders what the girl means.

Left. A burned-out bus in South London makes useful anti-strike propaganda.

Earls Court, the Empress Hall and the Queen's Hall by the Underground Railway Company and various bus companies. All the same, those people not involved directly in the strike had to get to work the best they could as there was not enough public transport available. However, there were the private cars of the rich always on hand for pretty young girls and there were lorries driven by public schoolboys who found it an exciting change from their ordinary training in their school Officers' Training Corps.

Exciting times, indeed. Stirring times for those who had missed the war or who had not joined the Black and Tans. Soldiers in battle order, armoured cars, police, specials in jodhpurs and plus fours and a strand or two of barbed wire draped here and there gave a truly martial atmosphere.

Truculent Churchill, editor of the Government news sheet, the *British Gazette*, lambasted the strikers, calling them the enemy; their supporters, Reds and all the other odds and sods within spitting distance. That included the B.B.C. whose news service under Reith seemed to be too impartial for him, despite the fact that the radio gave no coverage to trade union leaders.

But there were reports that the jolly old police were playing football matches with the strikers. To be sure, had this become a regular practice reports of such goings-on would have been suppressed. The authorities would never have encouraged fraternising. There were no reports, however, of the polo-playing specials playing a few chukkas with the strikers nor any reports of plus-fours garbed specials playing golf with the miners.

In nine days the strike was broken. The T.U.C. surrendered and the rest of the strikers deserted their miner comrades. It was on the understanding that the Government would start negotiations to settle the dispute, but the T.U.C. must have realised that would be unlikely. In fact nothing was settled. Unemployment rose, workers were victimised and people, lapsing deeper into poverty, went hungry. The miners struggled on hopelessly until November when, starved into submission, they began to drift back to the pits.

It was said that during the strike a quarter of a million men had joined the special constabulary and thousands more had volunteered to drive vehicles. Lord Winterton, Tory M.P. who had organised supplies for Oxfordshire and Buckinghamshire, wrote that on the last day of the strike he had ten thousand more volunteers than he could find work for and that one lot of "young wage earners", whatever that was supposed to mean, asked to be sent as special constables to Glasgow so that they could have a "crack at them dirty Bolshies on the Clyde." A likely story, but that "them" was, no doubt, thought to be a clever little touch. Authentic working class—very plausible. How many volunteers were there to work down the mines? It took conscription to get men down the mines in the second World War, when men preferred to take their chances in the fighting services.

Considering the passions, the actions and reactions at the time of the General Strike, the hardships of the strikers, especially the miners, the inconvenience to workers not on strike and the grim, unbending attitude of the Tory Government, as well as the mobilising of one half the country against the other, it is surprising how little violence there was. Police baton charges, certainly; a bus burned, a car or two overturned. Little violence but a lot of suffering, the brunt of it borne by the miners.

The miners had been defeated. They had seen how difficult it was to achieve solidarity with other workers. Too much had been stacked against them. So back they went to the pits; back to danger, lower wages and longer hours. It was a time they would never forget or forgive, whoever owned the pits—private enterprise or the State. They would not make the same mistakes again.

Above. A Government communiqué describes the Strike as an "organised attempt to starve nation," when it was Government policy to starve miners.

Opposite. The *British Worker* had some hopes of a fair deal for miners.

The hysterical *Daily Mail* announces the collapse of the strike as "Surrender of the Revolutionaries."

ORGANISED ATTEMPT TO STARVE THE NATION

Orders By Leaders Of The Railway And Transport Trade Unions.

SUBSTANTIAL IMPROVEMENT IN THE TRAIN SERVICES.

Government's New Steps To Protect The People.

SITUATION BECOMING MORE INTENSE.

OFFICIAL COMMUNIQUE.

May 7.

No serious disorder has occurred in any part of the country. The work of feeding the people and of maintaining light and power and essential communications is being successfully accomplished. Over 2,000 trains were run on May 6, or nearly double the day before.

A further substantial improvement both on the main lines and in the metropolitan and suburban services is arranged for to-day.

The protection of 'buses in London proved yesterday most satisfactory, and they are constantly increasing in numbers.

AUGUST, 1929

PRICE 1/- NET

The Boy's Own Paper

THE WORLD'S BEST MAGAZINE FOR BOYS

Popular reading throughout the 1920s was *The Boy's Own Paper,* aimed at school-boys of all ages. This issue, August, 1929, contained amongst other articles, 'How I Made a Sundial', 'A Boomerang Catapult', 'The Making of Strength (Pt. 2. The Legs)', and 'Damp-Proof Matches'.

THE
BRITISH WORKER

OFFICIAL STRIKE NEWS BULLETIN

Published by The General Council of the Trades Union Congress

No. 3.   WEDNESDAY EVENING, MAY 12, 1926.   PRICE ONE PENNY

STRIKE TERMINATED TO-DAY

Trades Union Congress General Council Satisfied That Miners Will Now Get a Fair Deal

HOW PEACE CAME

Telegrams Already Sent to All Unions Concerned to Instruct Their Branches at Once : Miners Call Delegate Conference

The General Strike is over.

The General Council of the Trades Union Congress proclaimed this to-day, having reached the conclusion, as a result of a number of conversations with Sir Herbert Samuel, that a satisfactory basis of settlement in the mining industry can now be formulated. The official announcement was issued by Mr. Arthur Pugh, after the General Council had been received this morning by Mr. Baldwin and a number of his Cabinet colleagues.

Telegrams of instruction have already been sent to all affiliated bodies.

The Miners' Federation Executive will report fully to a conference to be convened next Friday.

The negotiations which led to the termination of the general strike were facilitated by the intervention of Sir Herbert Samuel, the Chairman of the Coal Commission.

Sir Herbert returned specially from Italy, where he was

T.U.C. ORDER

In order to resume negotiations, the General Council decided to terminate the General Strike to-day.

Telegrams of instructions were sent to the Executive Committees of affiliated unions, who will communicate with the branches of their organisations, in accordance with their usual practice. Members before acting must wait definite instructions from their own Executive Councils.

taking a short vacation, to ascertain whether his services could be utilised towards resolving the differences between the parties.

A number of informal conversations took place between him and representatives of the General Council, as a result of which the General Council reached the conclusion that a satisfactory basis of settlement could be formulated.

The Memorandum and the correspondence which is published in this issue indicates, in the view of the General Council, the lines along which negotiations can proceed to effect a solution to the many problems which the situation in the Coal Mining Industry has given rise.

The proposals, if approached and operated in a spirit of whole-hearted co-operation between all parties concerned, should result in a more equitable and durable relationship than has hitherto existed in the Coal Mining Industry.

The Movement came out in order to ensure a fair deal for the Miners. They are satisfied that that can now be achieved.

The following letters have been exchanged between Sir Herbert-Samuel and the General Council of the Trades Union Congress :—

May 12th, 1926.

Dear Mr. Pugh,

As the outcome of the conversations which I have had with your Committee, I attach a memorandum embodying the conclusions that have been reached.

I have made it clear to your Committee from the outset that I have been acting entirely on my own initiative, have received no authority from the Government, and can give no assurances on their behalf.

I am of opinion that the proposals embodied in the Memorandum are suitable for adoption, and are likely to promote a settlement of the differences in the Coal Industry.

I shall strongly recommend their acceptance by the Government when the negotiations are renewed.

Yours sincerely,
(Signed) HERBERT SAMUEL.

CONTINUED ON PAGE FOUR

PLEASE PASS THIS ON.

Daily Mail.

PRICE ONE PENNY.   FOR KING AND COUNTRY.   THURSDAY, MAY 13th, 1926.

Surrender of the Revolutionaries.

T.U.C. STRIKE CALLED OFF UNCONDITIONALLY.

VICTORY FOR THE PEOPLE.

NEW COAL SETTLEMENT PLANS.

The General Council of the Trades Union Congress surrendered unconditionally yesterday, the ninth day of the General Strike.

The surrender took place at No. 10, Downing-street, the residence of the Prime Minister, following a con-

Mr. BALDWIN'S STATEMENT.

A Victory for Common Sense.
OVATION FOR THE PREMIER.
(*From the Parliamentary Correspondent.*)
HOUSE OF COMMONS, Wednesday.

The attendance of Socialist members was poor, and when the Prime Minister came in leading a small procession in which Mr. Winston Churchill the Chancellor and Sir William Joynson Hicks the Home Secretary were prominent figures, the Government supporters rose to their feet, waved their

LEADING ARTICLE.

FOR KING & COUNTRY.

Revolution Routed.

The general strike has been "officially called off." It has been called off because it signally failed in face of the unflinching determination of the British people. Its failure is one more victory for law and order. Sir John Simon dealt it the first heavy blow when he

What the miners went back to. Mine disaster in Ebbw Vale, 1927. Ambulances wait at the pithead.

Ebbw Vale: anxious relatives wait for news of entombed men.

The Lindy hop

WHEN CHARLES AUGUSTUS LINDBERGH LANDED AT LE BOURGET, Paris, on 21 May, 1927 there was a crowd of over 100,000 to meet him. My father was one of the crowd. He happened to be in Paris on business at the time and one of his associates, a coloured American comedian, had driven him to the airport. I had just "won a scholarship," as they used to say in those days, and was waiting until the next term to start grammar school.

To tell the truth, my friends and I were not very much impressed by Lindbergh's achievement. We were interested, of course, but our real heroes of the air were the fighter pilot aces of World War I—Barker, Bishop, Ball; Fonck, Guynemer, Nungesser; Richthofen, Boelcke and Immelman. Flying from A to B, no matter how far the distance, how hazardous the journey, did not seem to have the same impact as a dogfight over no-man's land with aerobatics, stuttering machine-guns and planes going down in flames. Aerial combat was what we found exciting and intriguing. We did not appreciate at the time Lindbergh's lone venture, the nearly forty gruelling hours of flying through bleak clouds and over the dark Atlantic Ocean, sometimes almost down to sea level with the chilling cold seeping into his flying suit; having to fight off sleep, with the ever present danger of crashing into the sea; being without radio contact with nobody to rely on but himself.

When my father returned from Paris a few days later he told us that he had actually seen the arrival of the plane, but he had not seen Lindbergh. He also said that he reckoned that his own drive back from Le Bourget to Paris had been a worse experience than Lindbergh's epic flight from New York.

Lindbergh was twenty-five years old when he made the first solo non-stop transatlantic flight from New York to Paris in his high-wing, single rotary engine monoplane, *Spirit of St. Louis*. During the two previous years he had been employed flying mail planes between St. Louis and

Chicago in all weathers and was an experienced aviator. He had attended the University of Wisconsin for two years before leaving to take flying lessons in Lincoln, Nebraska. While in Lincoln he had started a barn-storming career, wing-walking and parachute jumping, and had become known as the "flying fool." In 1924 he became a flying cadet in the U.S. Army Air Corps and was outstanding as a pupil. However, his penchant for playing practical jokes did not make him popular with his colleagues, especially as his jokes were apt to be very unfunny and sometimes bordered on the dangerous. Even when he had achieved his ambition to fly a mail plane, Lindbergh soon began to find it irksome and he longed to find a new outlet for his flying ability.

The first non-stop flight across the Atlantic had been in 1919 by two British flyers in an old Vickers Vimy bomber of World War I. Captain Alcock and Lieutenant Whitten Brown had left Newfoundland at tea time and had crash-landed in an Irish bog sixteen hours later. But until May 1927 nobody had made the solo flight across the Atlantic and Ortez was offering a prize of twenty-five thousand dollars for the first flight to be made from New York to Paris or vice-versa.

Lindbergh decided he would make the attempt, but he needed money to finance the project. There were other pilots who were in an advanced stage of preparation to make a bid for the prize but Lindbergh was undeterred. He looked around for backers and sponsors. They were not easy to find. Lindbergh realised that his best chance to succeed in his flight was to have a plane specially built to undertake the arduous task. In this he was lucky to find a company willing and capable of building the plane he wanted and within his budget. Rivals were experiencing setbacks and difficulties in their preparations as Lindbergh grimly stuck to his job. But just as Lindbergh was getting set for his flight, news arrived that the French flying aces, Nungesser and Coli, had set off from Le Bourget, Paris, bound for New York. It seemed as if Lindbergh had, after all, missed the plane, so to speak. However, one man's misfortune can turn out to be another's fortune. The two intrepid French airmen vanished over the Atlantic and were never seen again. Lindbergh decided there was no time to lose.

Without further delay, his *Spirit of St. Louis* was wheeled out of its hangar. Jostled by newspaper reporters, photographers and other hangers-on, young Lindbergh was pelted with question after question most of which he thought were stupid, trivial or irrelevant. However, he was soon on the first leg of his flight to New York, 2,400 miles to the north. His flight from St. Louis took just over twenty-one hours and was a record.

In New York Lindbergh was again besieged by the press and public relations people as further preparations were made for the Atlantic flight. Then, on the morning of May 20, 1927, Lindbergh's main backer, Harry Knight, gave him the thumbs up sign and wished him luck as he climbed into the open cockpit of the *Spirit of St. Louis*. The

News item the morning after Lindbergh's flight.

chocks were pulled away and the overloaded plane trundled across the soggy runway of Roosevelt Field and lurched away into mist and glory.

Charles Lindbergh touched down at Le Bourget, outside Paris, at 10.20 p.m. European time on Saturday May 21 after thirty-three and a half hours in the air. The crowd that greeted his arrival was hysterical and Lindbergh had to be spirited away. Herrick, the American ambassador, and staff of the U.S. Embassy were no less hysterical than the welcoming crowd. Herrick sent a telegram to Washington eulogising the "heaven-sent all-American." Showers of medals and accolades descended on the intrepid aviator.

As in Paris, wildly cheering crowds were waiting for Lindbergh when he arrived at Croydon on a visit to Britain. He met King George V, he hobnobbed with the Prince of Wales and other nobs and did his all-American bit. He was feted, wined and dined, but he was already beginning to find his new role irksome. The American press with its eye on the main chance, was clamouring for his return. He represented big news, big business, big money. Everyone with an axe to grind wanted to get in on the act, especially concerns such as Mobiloil and A.C. Sparking Plugs with whom Lindbergh had signed contracts. They wanted to cash in and so too, for that matter, did Lindbergh. He was no slouch himself when it came to turning a buck, but although he screwed the companies for the last dollar he was strict about the products he chose to endorse.

He returned to New York and was given the customary ticker-tape welcome reserved for heroes, and the full treatment. Gifts were homing in on him from practically every corner of the earth, from emperors, kings, big businesses, small businesses and private individuals. He received gifts ranging from large sums of money to small keepsakes. He was even awarded the Medal of Honour, usually reserved for wartime heroes, by his government.

In the summer of 1927 Lindbergh made an extensive tour of the United States in the *Spirit of St. Louis*. He was received everywhere with adulation but the circus was beginning to pall. The gilt was off the gingerbread. Lindbergh was becoming disenchanted with the public in general and their press representatives in particular. Nevertheless, he still kept his eye on the main chance. It would be some years before he would have to face tragedy and sorrow, some years before his flights into fields beyond his real capacity would tarnish his image as the all-American boy, some years before the story of the flying heroes who pioneered civil aviation between the wars would be dimmed by the sustained heroism of thousands and thousands of fliers in World War II.

Money to Burn

HEN WE WERE CHILDREN MY BROTHER AND I WOULD OFTEN go to the local sweetshop for a halfpenny lucky dip. This meant diving an arm into a barrel of sawdust and pulling out whatever gift came to hand, usually a sherbert dab, a few sweets wrapped in a coloured piece of paper or a small German toy wrapped in a genuine German note for a million marks or so. Such notes were, indeed, less than two a penny. Most children were ardent cigarette card collectors at the time and sometimes, if one was lucky, a young, not-so-knowledgable collector could be persuaded to part with one "Cries of London" or a couple of "Do You Knows" for one of these German notes. We knew, somehow, that these handsome looking notes had no more value than the paper they were printed on, without the vaguest idea of the appalling significance of this.

Years later, in Singapore just after the Japanese surrender in 1945, Japanese notes issued during the occupation were as worthless as those old German marks and one had to be extremely wary in dealing with the locals, not to be fobbed off with useless Japanese currency. The locals likewise were just as wary not to find themselves being paid for goods with such paper, by the "licentious" soldiery. However, I kept a few of the Japanese notes as souvenirs. I was stuck with them after a little cigarette transaction with a couple of Chinese in a dark alley off New Bridge Street, Singapore. Anyway, the carton of cigarettes I gave in exchange had a packet of cigarettes at each end only; in between was stuffed some old "four by two" rifle cleaning material. So I reckoned it was "Even Stephen" as only one of the notes I received in payment was genuine. I was reminded of the exchange of cigarette cards for German marks.

At the end of World War I Germany's international trade was completely out of balance. Without colonies, with huge areas of metropolitan territory occupied by the allies and the terrifying burden of

Millions of marks, so much rubbish. Germans sorrowfully survey the valueless notes.

reparations, Germany under the Weimar Republic faced economic and political chaos. This was heightened by the refusal of Poland to return Upper Siberia to Germany, in violation of the mandate of the plebiscite held in March 1921.

In 1914, at the outbreak of the war, the German mark was worth about 5p. By 1918 its purchasing had fallen to about 1½p. The depreciation of the currency continued at an ever-accelerating rate until it became a veritable landslide. By 1923 prices in German shops were

89

English newspaper posters sum up German inflation.

1,247,000 times higher than they had been in 1914, and prices were being raised in shops and restaurants at least twice a day. A person drawing his salary, which could be two suitcases full of high denomination notes, would find that by the time he had reached the bus stop he did not have enough money to pay his fare home. German notes for millions of marks were used in England as sweet wrappers.

Squabbles over German reparations to the allies had gone on since the peace treaty. Germany had been accused of engineering her currency decline in the early stages in order to avoid payment of reparations. Defaults in making these payments finally reached a head when France accused the Germans of cheating them in deliveries of coal and when Germany failed to supply France with 100,000 telegraph poles. In February 1923 fifty thousand French and Belgian troops with tanks and armoured cars marched in to occupy the Ruhr, the main industrial region of Germany. The German answer was a policy of passive resistance. The German government thought that in order to support this policy it must try to slow down the constant rise in the cost of living.

The authorities started to sell off some of their holdings in foreign currency and this policy was made easier because, as a result of the occupation of the Ruhr, reparation payments in cash had been suspended. But it soon became obvious that the halt in rising prices was only temporary. Ruhr industries had been shut down as part of the passive resistance and the dislocation in the collieries compelled Germany to place large contracts in England for coal which had to be paid for in sterling. The general interference with normal trade increased Germany's already excessive imports over exports. Foreigners were afraid to hold marks. Exchange rates soared. So did prices in the shops and they continued to soar. Members of the German public lost all confidence in their money and started to panic. The German government, finding that supporting the exchange rate would mean parting with the remainder of their rapidly dwindling foreign reserves, practically left the currency to its fate.

The government itself, with prices doubling and redoubling, could not pay its way with the revenue from taxes fixed months before and sought to borrow from the Reichsbank. The bank provided the money by simply printing more notes. In fact, printing presses were working at full capacity just printing marks. Old notes of low denominations such as ten and one hundred marks were useless for anything but scrap paper. Loads of these notes went to the incinerator and banks sold them by the truckload for pulping.

The mark had received a severe blow when a German court decided in the case of a debtor who contracted a debt when the value of the mark had been relatively high and had tried to settle the debt at face value with the depreciated mark notes. In Germany there was no legal distinction between the gold or the paper mark or between the various issues of the paper marks themselves and the debtor was technically

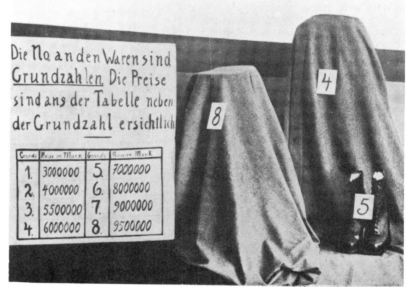

Die No. an den Waren sind Grundzahlen. Die Preise sind aus der Tabelle neben der Grundzahl ersichtlich

Grundz.	Preis in Mark	Grundz.	Preis in Mark
1.	3000000	5.	7000000
2.	4000000	6.	8000000
3.	5500000	7.	9000000
4.	6000000	8.	9500000

Above left. Berlin newspaper seller carries a basket full of millions of marks for loose change.

Top right. French occupation troops run a soup kitchen for Germans, on the Ruhr.

Centre right. Notice in Berlin shop window tells the story of runaway inflation.

German policeman stands behind a tip full of money to burn.

within his right to settle a debt for a thousand marks contracted when it had been worth say £100, with a note for that amount when it was practically worthless. But the court decided that a repayment of the debt with depreciated marks was inequitable. This ruling was not universally applied however, otherwise it would also have had to cover government debts.

Municipalities, industrial companies and even small private companies took to printing their own notes, some even using them to pay into their own bank accounts, then withdrawing an equivalent amount from another branch in official Reichbank notes to use to bid for foreign currency. This ploy sent the exchange rate soaring further and further out of control until talking of money in just millions became meaningless.

Of course, there were those who were able to profit from the situation. Business men borrowed capital from the banks as discounts and interest had no meaning with the value of money depreciating so rapidly. The result was that German industry was enabled to modernise itself at the expense of the nation's bank deposits.

With the exchange value of the mark being announced at eleven in the morning and again at five in the evening, most shopkeepers adjusted their prices accordingly. A person ordering a meal in a restaurant could well find that the price had doubled by the time he was presented with the bill. Panic spread and people scrambled to buy just about anything rather than hold on to money. Any shoddy item represented more stable value than a sackful of marks. Goods were bartered instead of being bought or sold. Workers were paid with sacks full of notes daily rather than weekly and, as they spent the money on anything rather than see its value melt away in a matter of hours, prices rose higher than ever.

German industry was working at full production, yet workers and their families were living in poverty for massive wage increases failed to keep up with the astronomical rise in prices. Using their own currency foreigners were able to buy goods and property for a song. People with small properties, finding themselves unable to cope with the cost of maintenance, sold them at ridiculous prices. Pensioners and people living on fixed incomes sold their jewellery, china, tableware and even clothing until they were destitute. Yet in the midst of all this misery there were big industrialists, speculators and profiteers living in absolute luxury.

But it was not these big operators who attracted the hatred of the masses. They were not as obvious to the man in the street as small operators and speculators in the markets and smaller shops and it was easy for the new National Socialist Party—the Nazis—to win support by directing attention on some small Jewish shop or speculator, then obliquely on to Jews in general.

Most of the speculators were not Jews anyway, but under the panic circumstances prevailing the Nazis created a convenient scapegoat for

Left. Butter before guns. Germans queue for butter in Berlin.

Right. French troops who marched into the Ruhr, man a check point.

suffering masses of German workers, in the main anti-Semitic at any time. Hitler used the situation to his advantage. He attacked the Weimar Republic and recruits flocked to join his storm troopers.

By the autumn of 1923 the situation in Germany was catastrophic although industry and agriculture were thriving. Farmers, rather than sell their products for useless stacks of paper, ate till bursting, bartered for their other needs at highly profitable terms, paid off their debts and mortgages, prospering while the country faced famine. Cruel selfishness and cynicism ate deeper and deeper into the fabric of the German nation personified in people such as Fritz Haarman, the homosexual detective, Nazi informer and mass murderer who operated a butcher business dealing in human carcases and did a thriving business in potted meats and secondhand clothes, and Denke, the quiet farmer who operated a similar business.

By October 1923 the crisis in the Reich was approaching its climax. Hitler was growing more strident and was waiting for his chance to pounce. In November the German finance minister called in Dr. Schacht and gave him the newly created post of Reichs Currency Controller. Dr. Schacht, as a private banker and manager of finances of the German occupation of Belgium, had shown dazzling brilliance. Now he acted swiftly and ruthlessly. He immediately stopped the private printing of money and set about introducing a new form of currency. Hitler and Ludendorff decided to act and made their abortive bid to seize power in Germany by force on November 8. By the next day the putsch had turned into a fiasco. This time the Nazis were thwarted and, on the day following, Schacht's new rentenmark was introduced.

The value of the rentenmark opened at 330,000 million old marks until it was stabilised by Schacht on November 20 at one billion old marks for one rentenmark. Galloping inflation in Germany was over, and for the next few years Germany experienced more or less normalcy in her economic condition. But her trials were really only just beginning.

93

Magic in the air

IN THE EARLY TWENTIES WHEN RADIO WAS WIRELESS, MY UNCLE, WHO was crippled and was bed-ridden for much of the time, was living with us. He was a keen wireless dabbler. First came the crystal sets with cat's whiskers; then it became more complicated. I never did know much about radio but I do remember some of the names my uncle used for the intricate mess of bits and pieces wired across a big table, and the headphones on which we could listen to crackling music and chat. There were rheostats, condensers, valves that lighted up, dull-emitters and alternators. I remember having to lug the dull yellowish, rubbery accumulator to a garage to be recharged, and I can still recall the smell of the acid.

Frankly, as kids, my brothers and I did not think the end result was worth all the trouble. We much preferred the cinema. Even the special programmes for children left us cold. After all, we found hanging on to one set of earphones between three of us not much in the way of entertainment, especially with all the fiddling and tuning and my uncle's constant mutterings about oscillation, atmospherics and frequencies, which were double-Dutch to us.

In the backyard, nailed to a brick wall, was a long wooden pole and an aerial extended from it to the roof of the house. Our neighbours were unimpressed and always feared it would attract lightning and that we would all be struck. It was not long before the aerial was dangling at various times our home-made handkerchief parachutes, conkers on string and a blue striped sock. I remember the sock because my mother said it did not come from anybody in our house.

However, things began to look up when a horn-shaped loudspeaker replaced the earphones and we could all listen in at the same time if we wanted to; but even so, as far as the family was concerned, the wireless was no great shakes. We could take it or leave it alone. For us, despite the novelty, most of the programmes, like the stuffed shirts of the period, were as boring as old boots. Those were the days.

94

On November 2, 1920 Station KDKA in Pittsburgh, U.S.A., broadcast a commentary on the election of Mr. Harding as President of the United States. The fact of the broadcast itself, if not the actual commentary, was received by an enraptured public. This new medium was to be no nine days wonder. Radio stations sprang up all over America and by August 1922 there were already sponsored programmes and millions of listeners.

At last, on November 14, 1922, the newly formed British Broadcasting Company relayed its first programme from the now famous London station 2LO on the top of Marconi House in the Strand—the news, at six o'clock. The Company, founded by the wireless manufacturing industry ostensibly as a public service, was dissolved in January 1927 and the British Broadcasting Corporation was constituted under a Royal Charter in its place.

Until January 1922, from Station 2MT, situated in an old army hut in the small Essex village of Writtle, the exuberant ex-R.F.C. Captain P. P. Eckersley had been broadcasting records and chat, showing the way to popular broadcasting. Eckersley, head of the Marconi design department, was Britain's first disc jockey. He was taken into the B.B.C. by Mr. Reith, its head, and in 1924 he actually designed the set presented to King George V by the B.B.C. But due to handicaps from outside and within the Corporation it was to be a long time before the B.B.C. was to deviate from its path of dinner-jacket philosophy of stereotyped boredom that accounted for so much of its broadcasting time before the last war.

One of the first B.B.C. announcers was Arthur Burrows who was in charge of the programme arrangements. Later, as "Uncle Arthur" of the Childrens' Hour, he was well-known to thousands of listeners. One of the first sports commentators was Jack Dempsey, then heavyweight champion of the world, who gave the commentary on the short-lived fight between Georges Carpentier and Kid Lewis in May 1922. His blow-by-blow account from the ringside at Olympia was telephoned to the *Daily Express* broadcasting station at Slough, the headquarters of their Radio Communication Company, and then sent out to the world.

The voices of well-known personalities came floating into homes all over Britain. There were George Robey, Stainless Stephen, H. G. Wells, Bernard Shaw and G. K. Chesterton, as well as religious speakers. If the programmes were mostly dull, what did it matter? Wireless was still a novelty and not yet a medium for the masses. But rapid changes were taking place. Radio was creating its own stars. There was Our Lizzie (Helen Millais), John Henry (the henpecked husband) and Blossom; Mabel Constanduros and Michael Hogan in the Buggins sketches; Willy Rouse as Wireless Willy, Bertha Wilmot, Wish Wynn, Norman Long and Tommy Handley with his 'Disorderly Room' sketch of the Roosters' Concert Party of the First World War; Vivian Foster (the Vicar of Mirth), Clapham and Dwyer and Nosmo King who had taken his name from a "No Smoking" sign.

Leslie Harrison Lambert, a senior Civil Servant whose pen-name was A. J. Allen, was popular as a storyteller in 1924, and during 1924 and 1925 over one hundred and forty plays were broadcast with such stars as Lewis Casson, Sybil Thorndike, Catherine Nesbitt and Gladys Cooper. Concerts broadcast from Covent Garden were conducted by Sir Hamilton Harty, Richard Strauss, Elgar and Siegfried Wagner. In 1924 the famous American coloratura singer, Madame Galli-Curci, came to Britain for a six weeks tour for a fee of £20,000. She was one of the singers whose records were being regularly broadcast. For just a small licence fee, listeners could relax in their own homes and listen to this highly paid star. They could also hear the voices of Caruso and Chaliapin and listen to a piano recital by Paderewski from Savoy Hill. There was magic in the air.

But the use of radio as a powerful means of propaganda was imminent. In the electioneering of 1924, leaders of the three main parties were given facilities to use broadcasting for the first time, although it was only Stanley Baldwin who delivered a special address directly into a microphone at the Savoy Hill headquarters of the B.B.C. It seemed he was relaxed and at ease with the new medium. Mr. Asquith, the Liberal leader, speaking from Scotland came over the air clear enough, but Ramsay MacDonald, the Labour leader, addressing an audience from a platform in a hall, was fidgety and careless of the microphone and any technique. His radio performance was poor and inept and did nothing to help the cause of the Labour Party, any more than did his strange reticence over the fraudulent Zinoviev letter.

An incident which indicated the growing power of broadcasting was in April 1926, a month before the General Strike was due to take place. Balliol scholar Father Ronald Knox broadcast a fictitious account of unemployment riots in which eye-witnesses gave accounts of attacks on the Houses of Parliament and people being burned alive in Trafalgar Square. Even if this did not create as big a panic as did Orson Welles later, with his famous broadcast of a Martian invasion in New York, nevertheless hundreds of people phoned to Savoy Hill, believing that the Houses of Parliament had really been attacked and revolution was imminent.

In 1925 the B.B.C. had opened the first and most powerful longwave transmitter in the world at Daventry. It meant a national network covering, in fact, eighty-five per cent of the country. So in the General Strike, when most newspapers ceased publication, restrictions were lifted on the context and timing of B.B.C. news bulletins. People who had never listened much to the radio before, now listened to the news. The B.B.C. claimed it adopted an independent, unbiased view at all times, but it was a case of radio news or no news. Split or bust. If the news was, indeed, impartial, the upper crust voices of the newscasters of the time made impartiality suspect to most strikers and their sym-

A contemporary cartoon of Sybil Thorndike by clever cartoonist Tom Titt.

Movies of the Twenties: Douglas Fairbanks and
Billy Dove in *Black Pirate* (Allied Artists), 1927.
The film was made in black-and-white, and this
still was hand-tinted (probably by the
projectionist at a local cinema!).

Movies of the Twenties: Ronald Colman and Lily
Damita in *The Rescue* (United Artists), 1927.
Another hand-tinted still from an original
black-and-white film.

Mr. and Mrs. Jack Hylton stand proudly alongside their new Lanchester Coupé in 1927.

The first issue of *Radio Times*, September 1923.

pathisers.

An early development of broadcasting had been the production of the B.B.C.'s own periodical, the *Radio Times*. London newspapers had refused to publish radio programmes unless they were paid for, like advertisements. For a while London programmes appeared in the advertisement columns of Selfridges in the *Pall Mall Magazine*. The newspapers had then lifted their embargo but in September 1923 the first issues of the *Radio Times* appeared and the print run of 250,000 copies was completely sold out. In January 1929 the B.B.C. published the first number of *The Listener*.

Radio concert parties were fashionable, with the Cooptimists and Radio Radiance leading the way, and the popularity of dance bands grew and grew. Millions listened to the Savoy Orpheans, and Carrol Gibbons, Jack Hylton and Sidney Firmin became household words. In 1928 the London Radio Dance Band, with Jack Payne, became the first B.B.C. dance orchestra. Cinema organists such as Reginald Foort had their day as well as string quartets, quintets and octets playing what was called light music, and the coloured duo, Layton and Johnstone sang just about anything that was singable. Albert Sandler conducted the first Palm Court broadcast from the Grand Hotel, Eastbourne, in 1925, setting a fashion, and band leader Christopher Stone became the first B.B.C. disc jockey.

Culture, it was early decided by Reith, was what the public needed, so the public was dished out great globs of glutinous concoctions, much of it by innovators experimenting with new techniques. How many listeners wanted Pirandello's *The Man with a Flower in his Mouth?* All the same a lot of the programmes were acceptable to a wide range of the public, although a lot of programmes meant just an earache for most.

97

The broadcast of sports and outside events became possible with the B.B.C.'s Royal Charter in 1927. The lifting of restrictions on news and running commentaries was implicit in the Charter and for the first time major sports events such as the Cup Final, the Boat Race, Test matches and horse racing classics were allowed. Until the Charter, opposition to such broadcasts had been mainly from newspaper proprietors and sports and entertainments promoters.

But for many people it was still a case of the rough having to be taken with the smooth. A lot of broadcasting time was taken up with schools programmes, talks on music appreciation, chamber music which was anathema to millions, and erudite talks. The British public had not yet had its fill of sport, music hall variety shows, dance band music and plays which they could understand. The public at large was not really ready for the B.B.C.'s cultural crusade. Popular brain fodder, in the shape of programmes like *The Brains Trust*, had yet to come. At all times the B.B.C. came in for plenty of stick one way or another, not that it always made a lot of impression in the Corporation. In 1925 when there were some objections to jokes made by comedians, a directive was issued to broadcasters banning jokes about drink, afflictions, parson sand one or two races of people. Some people were furious about dull Sundays when the air became holy and charged with funereal music and sombre dronings. Broadcasters had not yet learnt how to dress up religious programmes with wraps of popular songs and stars on Sunday.

There were people who objected to the smarmy exaggerated upper-class accents of announcers, known as the B.B.C. accent; there were people who did not like the way the B.B.C. ducked objective programmes on controversial subjects such as politics and religion. There are always objectors to anything, but it seemed that, too often, those with minority viewpoints were to be found in positions in the B.B.C. where they were able to force their ideas on a large public who suffered them as a cross that had to be borne in exchange for some radio entertainment.

However, one thing is for certain. Nowadays, those people who cannot go from one room to another without the radio switched on, who cannot drive a car without a blaring radio and those who walk blissfully through city streets with a transistor radio glued to the earhole, are not listening to *Thought for Today* or *Today in Parliament*. But, of course, nowadays the B.B.C. no longer has a monopoly as it did in the twenties. There are still some people who say, "More is the pity."

Scarface

WHEN I WAS A BOY I KNEW A BOY NAMED PHILLIPS WHOM I DID NOT like very much. He was always telling people to drop dead. He told me that his uncle was Jack "Legs" Diamond, a notorious New York gangster, so I told him that my uncle was Al Capone. It was like saying my uncle was the champ. So we had a fight and he told me to drop dead.

Some years ago when I was in Boston, Mass., I met a man who had a candy outlet near the hotel where I was staying. We became friendly. He told me he had driven a beer truck for Capone back in the twenties and had been hijacked twice and shot twice. He showed me the bullet scars to prove it. He said he had only spoken to Capone once. Driving a beer truck was like driving a truck for any big trucking company; you do not often get to talk to the boss. I asked my friend what he had felt about hauling booze in those days. He shrugged and said it was a living. He laughed and went on to say that he had never been a drinking man at the best of times and that the old prohibition days certainly had not been the best of times for drinking, anyway. He said he had always wondered what the big deal was, that so many folk had been prepared to break the law where liquor was concerned and would drink any old rotgut rather than go without. Everyone in those days referred to his bootlegger in much the same way as one refers to his doctor, solicitor or bookmaker.

One afternoon, just before Halloween, I happened to be in the candy store buying a stock of prepared candies for the young "trick or treat" merchants, when a policeman walked in. The storekeeper, with a wide grin, introduced him to me as his son. The son, whose name was Brian, asked me what part of England I came from. I told him London and he asked me if I knew Lincoln. He had been in the United States Air Corps and had been stationed near there at one time. We talked about violent crime for a while and I said I was surprised he was not wearing a pistol. He showed me that he did, in fact, carry a pistol inside his coat. He asked me if I would like to visit a small museum of crime exhibits and I said I would.

The next day I met Brian outside the Prudential Building on Boylston

Street and he took me to a large closed truck with several windows which was parked nearby. It was a mobile museum of crime and the exhibits in the interior included a half size mock-up of a death cell, a large collection of pistols, zip guns, coshes and some gory pictures. While we were inside the truck several youths came in to look at the exhibits. They did not appear too happy with what they saw and I remarked upon this. Brian told me that one of the ideas of the mobile museum was to impress the youngsters that crime did not pay by showing them gruesome pictures of hoodlums who had been killed in the streets in "shoot-outs" with the police.

Brian and I then went into a drugstore for coffee. We spoke about his dad and I mentioned what he had told me of his old bootlegging days. Brian grinned and said I could take much of what his dad said with a big pinch of salt and as for the bullet scars, sometimes his father said he had received the wounds while serving with the Marines in Nicaragua, which, said Brian, was really remarkable on account that his father had never been in the Marines, nor had he ever been to Nicaragua or anywhere else outside the States, for that matter.

Brian looked at me for a moment, then said, "To tell the truth, it was my Uncle Ed who drove the beer truck for Capone; my dad just drove a furniture removal truck for Irving Katz, his sister's father-in-law."

Al Capone was born in Brooklyn in 1899 and while still in his early teens attracted the attention of "Terrible Johnny Torrio," a Neopolitan gangster. Sponsored by Torrio, seventeen years his senior, Capone joined the "Five Pointers," a notorious Manhattan gang. Later he was hired by Frankie Uale, known as Yale, as a bouncer at the gangster's Harvard Inn. It was during a fracas at the inn that Capone received the knife scars that earned him the nickname Scarface, a name copied by the Press, which he hated. He boasted that he had been wounded while serving in France during the war but he had never even been drafted. In 1918 he married an Irish girl and, when they had a son, Torrio was the godfather.

Torrio went to work full time as business manager for his uncle, "Big Jim" Colosimo, at his nightclub in Chicago, and he soon sent for Capone. Capone, then in deep trouble with the New York police, lost no time in joining his sponsor, taking his wife and son with him. That was in 1919 and the young hoodlum was given a job at Colosimo's new Four Deuces, an establishment which combined offices, saloon, gambling rooms and a brothel. Capone's job was combination chauffeur, bodyguard, bartender, bouncer and tout for the brothel. It did not seem that way but Capone was heading for the big time.

On January 17, 1920 the National Prohibition Act came into effect. Generally manufacturing and supplying liquor under this act, known as the Volstead Act, was illegal, and gangsters were ready for this golden opportunity to take over supplying the huge demand for alcoholic drinks. Within an hour of the bill coming into force the gangsters were in motion, raiding and hijacking assignments of whisky earmarked for medicinal purposes. On May 11, 1920 Colosimo was shot dead in the foyer of his restaurant and Torrio took over. It was suspected that Torrio, at Capone's instigation, had hired Frankie Yale from New York to do the job, but many believed that Capone himself was the killer. However, no arrests were made and Torrio and Capone began to expand their interests in the face of increasing competition from rival gangs operating all over Chicago staking out claims to territory for their operations.

On the North side Dion O'Banion, a quick tempered killer who controlled the Irish vote, had in the field a formidable array of gunmen. He had an interest in a flower shop opposite Notre Dame Cathedral, where as a boy he had sung in the choir. He cornered the market supplying wreaths for gangsters' lavish funerals, and no doubt supplied the corpses too on a number of occasions. His lieutenants were Earl "Little Hymie" Weiss, "Schemer" Drucci, Bugs Moran who was a Pole, Louis Alterie, known as Two Gun Louis, and Samuel Morton, who had served in World War I as a first lieutenant.

On the West side, the O'Donnell brothers, William (Klondike), Miles and Bernard led an all-Irish gang. Between Little Italy and Cicero, Terry Druggan and Frank Lake ran the Valley Gang.

Joe "Hop Toad" Giunta, the joker.

Little Italy, on the South side, was in the hands of the "Terrible" Gennas, six villainous brothers, all swarthy, jet haired and jet eyed. Notorious members of their gang were John Scalise, who was tall, and his close companion Albert Anselmi who was short and fat, Samoots Amatuna and "Scourge" Tropea. In 1920 the Gennas had a licence for handling industrial alcohol. They used it as a basis for their illegal whisky, redistilling it and colouring it. They had the local Sicilians hard at work distilling liquor in bathtubs in their own homes. The local fixer who helped the Gennas was "Diamond Joe" Esposito.

Another South side gang was predominantly Irish, Ragen's Colts, and had originally started as a baseball team. The members of the gang professed to be all-American and were racist in character.

On the far South side the O'Donnell brothers, Ed "Spike", Steve, Walter and Tommy, reigned. They were no relations of the West side O'Donnells. The South West side was controlled by the Saltis-McErlane gang. Joe Saltis was a Pole, as was a lieutenant, John "Dingbat" O'Berta. Frank McErlane was an alcoholic and a compulsive killer. He was the first gangster to use a Thompson sub-machine gun.

For nearly three years Torrio managed to keep the peace between

The end of "Big Jim" Colisimo. Having Capone for a bodyguard did not save him.

the rival gangs as they milked their territories. He made Capone manager of the Four Deuces, and within a couple of years made him a full partner in all their operations. Capone opened a secondhand furniture shop as a blind, next to the Four Deuces. He brought his brothers to Chicago and later Ralph Capone rose to command level.

In 1922 Capone, on a drunken jaunt, crashed into a parked car injuring the driver. Capone brandished a revolver and threatened everyone in sight. He was arrested and charged, but not only were the charges dropped, they were expunged from the records. Capone was beginning to make his power felt.

In the summer of 1923, Spike O'Donnell, who had been in Joliet Prison, was released. He was far from satisfied with Torrio's policy of fair shares for all. He imported New York hoodlums, notably Harry Hasmiller, and began to hijack Torrio's beer trucks. Moreover his salesmen, George "Sport" Bucher and George Meeghan forced the sale of O'Donnell beer in Torrio and Saltis territory.

But a new threat was posed to the gangsters when Mayor Thompson was defeated at the elections and reformist Derwent William E. Dever was voted in. His chief of police, Morgan A. Collins, cracked down hard, closing gambling establishments including the Four Deuces.

Capone chose Cicero, a suburb of Chicago, as a new centre of operations. The growing syndicate included Ralph and Frank Capone, the Fischettis, the Gusiks, the La Cava brothers (Louis and Joesph), Pete Penovitch, Jimmy Mondi, Tony "Mops" Volpi, Pete Payette, Louis Consentino, Frank "the Enforcer" Nitti and Frankie Pope. Dion O'Banion became an associate in the gambling and brewery operations.

In 1923 Torrio went off on a tour of Europe leaving Capone in charge, established at the Hawthorne Inn headquarters in Cicero. The place was like a fortress with steel shutters and an extensive armoury. From this stronghold Capone directed operations until Torrio returned from Europe in 1924 in time for the new elections. It was in the gangsters' interests to defeat the Democrats and Capone made sure that defeated they would be. His gangsters patrolled the town in a fleet of large cars, terrorising the voters. Recalcitrant voters were beaten up, kidnapped and killed. Two men were shot dead near the Hawthorne, a man had his throat slit and another was killed in a saloon. The Chicago police were called out and fought pitched battles with the gangsters in the streets. The climax was a shoot-out with Al Capone, Frank Capone and Fischetti. Frank was killed, Fischetti arrested, but Al got away. Fischetti was soon released. Frank was buried with huge ceremony. Flowers, of course, were supplied by O'Banion.

On September 7, 1924, the beer war really started. Three of the O'Donnell brothers from the South side together with three of their men, Meeghan, O'Connors and Bucher, visited the speakeasy run by Jacob Geis as an exercise in intimidation. They knocked out Geis and beat up bartenders but three McErlane hoodlums led by Danny McFall had been following them. The O'Donnells went on to Klepka's Bar where Spike joined them and then the McErlanes struck. O'Connors was shot dead; the O'Donnells got away.

Ten days later, Bucher and Meeghan, driving two truckloads of beer, were held up and blasted by Frankie McErlane and Danny McFall with shotguns. In December two more O'Donnell men were held up. One was killed. The next victim was Phil Corrigan, shot at the wheel of another O'Donnell truck. Later Harry Hasmiller was killed in a run-

Capone is unperturbed when questioned about his bootlegging and other activities.

104

Left. George "Bugs" Moran, lucky to escape the St. Valentine Day massacre.

Right. Dion O'Banion, who shook hands with death in his own flower shop.

ning fight with a Saltis-McErlane group.

In September 1925 Spike narrowly escaped death when McErlane, using a Tommy-gun for the first time, fired at him from a car. A month later, in another attempt, Tommy O'Donnell was wounded. Spike, realising that his organisation was no match for the Torrio-Capone combination, fled to New York. Capone was placed at the scene of gang killings but the police were unable to proceed with charges against him. Torrio and Capone expanded their business in every direction without hindrance from the police or rival gangsters. Capone seemed immune from police interference. In fact, when in front of witnesses he had shot dead a freelance hijacker who had insulted his old friend, Jake "Greasy Thumb" Guzik, Capone went free.

In May 1924 O'Banion had offered to sell his brewery to Torrio and Capone and retire. They agreed to O'Banion's terms but not only did he double-cross them by tipping off the police, but bragged about it. His doom was sealed. When Mike Merlo, head of the Unione Siciliane, died in November, Yale took over. Merlo was to be given the usual funeral in the gangster tradition and wreaths and floral arrangements were ordered by the dozen from O'Banion's flower store. Two days after Merlo's death three men came into the store to order a wreath and shot O'Banion dead. The O'Banions suspected that Scalise, Anselmi and Yale had been the killers, and Hymie Weiss, who took over the leadership of the gang, swore vengeance.

In January 1925 Capone was driven to a restaurant. He entered, leaving the chauffeur and two bodyguards sitting in the car. Suddenly a large black car drew alongside, raking it with gunfire and killing the chauffeur. The assailants were Hymie Weiss, Schemer Drucci and Bugs Moran. Capone next ordered a custom built armoured car from Cadillac. Then Capone's new chauffeur-bodyguard was kidnapped, brutally tortured, shot dead and crammed into a water tank in a belt of woods. There was no doubt that O'Banion men had been responsible.

The St. Valentine massacre.
Scene of carnage after a
Capone execution squad had
"taken care" of the Moran
gang.

Torrio, who had been away from Chicago on holiday, returned to face the brewery charge. He opted to go to jail and safety while Al resolved the Weiss threat. But before he could arrange it, Torrio, who had been on a shopping expedition, was going towards his home when two men jumped from a car, guns blazing. He was blasted by another two men from inside the car. Torrio was taken to hospital where he recovered, but he was glad to go to prison for the next nine months. He transferred everything to Capone and retired from the scene. Capone knew he was in for a battle for survival; he must now subjugate or wipe out every major gang in Chicago. He realised the importance of maintaining fit soldiers. He urged his men to train in the well-equipped gymnasium he had built and made them practise with their firearms. He even tried to make his men get more sleep and drink less. The bloodiest and longest gang war ever fought in Chicago was about to break out with Irish, Polish and Jewish gangs aligning themselves with the O'Banions. The West side O'Donnells and later, Saltis-McErlane, went over to Weiss; Italians and Sicilians rallied to Capone and so did Druggan, Lake and Sheldon.

Capone's gang was extremely well organised in its administration as well as in the field. Some of the most dangerous gunmen in America were on his payroll and included such men as Samuel McPherson, "Golfbag" Hunt, Tony Accardo, the psychopath Sam Giancanna, "Camel" Humphries, "Machine-gun" Jake McGurn (whose real anme was De Mora) and his own favourite bodyguard, Phil D'Andrea. A well known sports outfitter, Fritz Von Frantzius, was his armourer. Joseph Klenha, Cicero's mayor, was nothing more than a stooge for Capone. Once Capone was seen to knock him down the steps of the Town Hall and put the boot in for good measure.

On the morning of May 25, 1925, Angelo Genna, newly married, was driving to view a newly acquired house when he was overtaken by a car driven by Frank Gusenberg. In the car were Weiss, Moran and Drucci, the old firm. Terrified, Genna accelerated in a desperate effort to escape, mounted the sidewalk and hit a lamp post. The three men in the pursuing car blasted him with sawn-off shotguns.

The O'Banions approached Samoots Amatuna to "set up" Scalise and Anselmi for them. He agreed but arranged to double-cross them. At the appointed time, Moran and Drucci were waiting in their car when another car drove by. In it were Scalise, Anselmi and Mike Genna and they opened fire, wounding both Moran and Drucci. A police car spotted the assailants speeding away and gave chase. They overtook the gangsters and detectives ordered them from the car. The gangsters answered with shotguns, killing the detectives. More police arrived and took up the pursuit of the fugitives. Mike Genna was killed but Scalise and Anselmi got away. That was on June 13.

On July 8, Tony Genna was "set up" by a disgruntled member of his own gang, named Giuseppe Nerone. He met Tony by arrangement and shook hands with him, but he clasped Genna's hand tightly as another man stepped from the shadows and shot Tony dead. The killer was "Schemer" Drucci, a Capone executioner. Nerone was shot dead later in a barber shop, but the surviving three Gennas were demoralised. They fled the Chicago battlefield and went into the import business. The next president of the Unione Siciliane, however, was not Capone nominee Lombardo, but Samoots Amatuna, who brazenly walked into the Unione headquarters with his bodyguards, "Bummy" Goldstein and Eddy Zion, and took over.

Anselmi and Scalise were arrested for the killing of the detectives in July and, despite wholesale intimidation of witnesses, were convicted. But appeals were made and Capone's full weight was behind them.

In late October Torrio was released from jail and Capone escorted him to safety. Torrio went to Italy. It was still not safe for him on the streets of Chicago and Capone had a lot of work to do. On November 13, Amatuna was sitting in a barber shop in Cicero when two men walked in and shot him dead. The two men were "Schemer" Drucci and Jim Flaherty. Three days later, on the way back from attending Amatuna's funeral, Eddie Zion was ambushed and gunned down, and two weeks after that, "Bummy" Goldstein met his death in a drugstore. Thus Lomardo became president of the Unione Siciliane.

At the end of 1925 Capone took his son to New York to see an ear specialist. On Christmas Eve Al went to the Adonis Club to drink with some old friends. Al claimed he was "set up." In a fracas three gangsters were shot dead. Capone was arrested then released on bail.

In Chicago, led by Tropea, a money raising campaign for the defence of Scalise and Anselmi was proceeding apace with threats and intimidation. Henry Springola, brother-in-law of Angelo Genna, was mown down by gunmen in a car driven by Baldelli. Then the brothers

left. John Scalise, Capone executioner executed by Capone.

right. Colisimo's was Chicago's plushiest pleasure palace, despite its outward appearance.

108

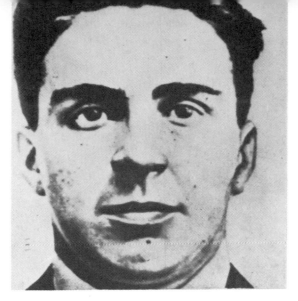

Left. Vincent "Schemer" Drucci, who was buried with military honours.

Right. Hymie Weiss, O'Banion stalwart ambushed by Capone murder squad.

Agostino and Antonio Morici were cut to pieces by blasts fired from the same car by the Anselmi-Scalise fund-raisers.

Retaliation was swift. On February 15, 1926, the "Scourge" Tropea was walking in the street, when he received the full charges of two shotguns that almost cut him in two. Nine days later, Baldelli accomplice Vito Bascone was found dead in a ditch with a bullet between the eyes and an index finger shot off, and at the bottom of a quarry not far away Baldelli's wrecked car was found. That same night Baldelli himself was found, dumped on an ashcan in an alley in North Chicago. He had been beaten and kicked, hacked and shot dead.

Capone's relations with the West side O'Donnells had deteriorated. The O'Donnells had been moving into Capone territory and openly boasted of selling beer there. One night Capone got word that they were at Harry Madigan's Pony Inn in Cicero and Capone decided to strike. He ordered a five car motorcade to locate the O'Donnells. Capone, carrying a machine gun, led the expedition. The O'Donnells and their companions were seen leaving the Inn and crossing the street toward their parked car and the Capone gang opened fire. As luck would have it, Myles and Klondyke O'Donnell were not hit, but their companions were terribly injured. One of them, Duffy, was left propped against a tree and the O'Donnells took the other two to Klondyke's house, but they were dead on arrival. The O'Donnells dumped the bodies which were soon discovered. One of them was identified as Doherty and the other as William A. McSwiggin, the young assistant States' attorney, despite the fact that all identifying marks had been removed from the clothing.

McSwiggin's father named Capone, Frank Rio, Frank Diamond and Bob McCullough as the killers. Capone denied having had any part in the crime, hinting that the assistant attorney was "on the take" anyway. The fact that the popular young McSwiggin had been consorting with gangsters shocked Chicago's citizens who were not easily shocked, but the fact that a state attorney had been shot down like any gangster angered them more. They started clamouring for action.

Al and his brother Ralph, as well as Charlie Fischetti, Pete Payette,

109

Al Capone in his prime, with Chicago in his pocket, had plenty to smile about.

Right. Tony Accardo in 1963; he followed Frank Nitti as mob boss.

Below. Albert Anselmi, cold-blooded execution partner of Scalise.

the three O'Donnells and Harry Madigan were arrested and charged with conspiracy to violate the Volstead Act. But later, they were all released and the McSwiggin Case was never resolved.

On August 6, 1926, Joe Saltis and Frank "Lefty" Koncil shot down John "Mittens" Foley, a member of the Sheldon gang. The Sheldon gang had been selling beer in Saltis-McErlane territory. The two killers were indicted. Then on August 10 Weiss and Drucci had to go to the Standard Oil Company building to keep an appointment. As they started to walk towards the building four gunmen ran across the street in their direction. Weiss and Drucci took cover behind a parked car and a pitched battle developed. Passers-by rushed for safety as police arrived on the scene. Three of the assailants got away but one, Louis Barko, a Capone triggerman, was caught. Weiss disappeared into the office building and Drucci was dragged by the police from the running board of a car as he tried to flee. Both men denied they had been involved in a gang battle and were released. Then on August 15 Weiss and Drucci were driving past the Standard Oil building when a car rammed them and bullets started to fly. The two men leaped from the car and raced into the building for protection.

On September 20 Weiss and his gang struck back. Capone and Frankie Rio, his lieutenant, were dining in the crowded restaurant of the Hawthorne Inn in Cicero when ten cars drove slowly past the windows, one behind the other, gunmen sending blast after blast of machine gun fire into the restaurant. Of the Capones, only Louis Barko, just entering the restaurant, was hurt. Weiss, Drucci, Bugs Moran and the Gusenberg brothers were suspected of the attack but nothing could be proved.

By this time Capone was beginning to realise that the internecine warfare was unprofitable and on October 4 proposed that Lombardo mediate a truce. However, Weiss made his main condition for peace the liquidation of Scalise and Anselmi and this Capone was not prepared to consider.

On October 11 Weiss, with two of his bodyguards, Sam Peller and Paddy Murray, Benny Jacobs a private investigator, and William W. O'Brien, a well-known criminal lawyer, got out of a car outside Notre Dame Cathedral and started to walk across to the O'Banion flower shop, above which Hymie Weiss had his headquarters. Machine guns opened up from the windows of a rented house where an ambush had been carefully prepared. Weiss and Peller were killed. As usual, Capone denied all knowledge of the affair and no action was taken against him by the police. But the death of Weiss revealed that the O'Banions were making tentative deals with Saltis and McErlane. Saltis became nervous of Capone's reactions and at his instigation a peace conference was called; rival gangs met at the Hotel Sherman and a reapportioning of territories was worked out.

On December 24, 1926 Anselmi and Scalise were released on bail

Johnny Torrio, sly ruthless schemer and Capone's sponsor. Although shot he survived to live out his days.

Right. Tony Accardo, prime suspect in the St. Valentine massacre.

from jail and it looked as though the new year would, at least, start peacefully. In fact, Al Capone was very expansive about the prospects. However, on December 30 it seemed that the ceasefire was over when Hilary Clements was blasted by a shotgun. He had been a beer-runner for Harry Sheldon and was caught selling beer in Saltis-McErlane territory. Instead of referring the affair to arbitration in the manner which had been decided at the Hotel Sherman, Saltis ordered the slaying of Clements. Sheldon protested to Capone and the result was that two Saltis-McErlane gangsters, Koncil and Hubacek, were executed on March 11, 1927.

But the O'Banions were not content with keeping the peace. On January 6, 1927 Capone was eating in Anton's, a favourite restaurant of his, when Anton was snatched in the vestibule. His body was later found buried in quicklime. He had been tortured and shot. In March, while on holiday in Hot Springs, Drucci failed in an attempt to shoot Capone.

Drucci was becoming desperate and it was whispered that he was growing more and more unstable. Election day in Chicago was not far off and all Chicago gangs were backing Thompson. Drucci led a raid on the offices of Crowe, a Dever stalwart, wrecked the place and beat up a secretary. Drucci was picked up by the police, became obstreperous, and was shot dead by a detective. He was buried with full military honours by the American Legion to which he belonged. Capone, who was at the graveside, smirked as a bugler played "taps."

Thompson was re-elected as Mayor of Chicago on April 5 and the city was to know an era of lawlessness worse than it had ever known before. Capone extended his headquarters and the Hotel Metropole became a den of iniquity with liquor, gambling and women available to gangsters, crooked politicians and police. Capone was riding higher than ever.